EXPLORING
NORTHUMBRIA

Kielder Water

EXPLORING NORTHUMBRIA

George Collard

Illustrated by Bernard Taylor and Iain Traill-Stevenson

ALAN SUTTON
1988

ALAN SUTTON PUBLISHING
BRUNSWICK ROAD · GLOUCESTER

First published 1988

British Library Cataloguing in Publication Data

Collard, George
Northumbria.
1. North-east England. Description & travel
I. Title
914.28'04858

ISBN 0-86299-474-8·

Typesetting by
Alan Sutton Publishing

Colour Reproduction by
Spa Graphics Limited, Cheltenham

Printed in Great Britain by
Guernsey Press Company Limited,
Guernsey, Channel Islands

To Jane and Ernie, my Northumbrian friends

ACKNOWLEDGEMENTS

I am grateful to Bernard Taylor and Iain Traill-Stevenson for the illustrations, without which this book would be nothing, also to Richard Metcalfe of Durham University, who has given invaluable help in the research and field work.

My wife, Nan, produced the maps, wrote out the music, typed the manuscript, corrected the mistakes and kept the enthusiasm going.

Peter Clifford of Alan Sutton Publishing supplied the confidence and encouragement.

FOREWORD

Northumbria is a real, living, breathing place, today more crowded with history and heritage than it is with people. It contains the most extensive National Nature Reserve Area of Outstanding Natural Beauty in England. It is contained within some of the least spoilt coastline and the best open moorland in Europe.

This living beauty is complimented by an introduction which invites you to come and spend time and see it all for yourself. It contains a wealth of local knowledge well laced with poetry, prose and song and with pictures that explore the essence of this country. The book invites you to know the Kingdom which welcomes you and yet demands that you leave only footprints and take only photographs and the products of the many local crafts.

David Bellamy
Bedburn 1988

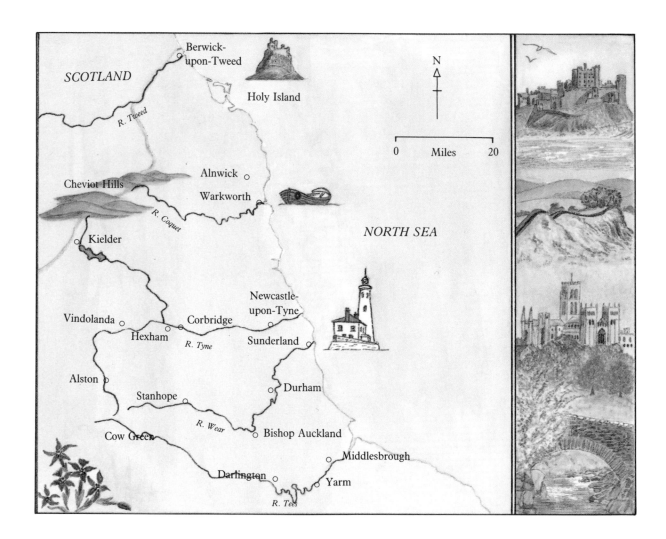

NORTHUMBRIA

CONTENTS

Croft Bridge

INTRODUCTION

The Saxon Kingdom of Northumbria stretched from the River Humbra (Humber) to the Forth. Now, however, the term is used to denote the old counties of Durham and Northumberland betwixt the Tees and the Tweed, once known as Berenice. It is an area steeped in history and grandeur, with vast expanses of moorland and forest designated as areas of outstanding natural beauty – yet the old kingdom must be one of the least known areas in England.

Once the scene of skirmishes and battles between the English, Scots and Romans, saints and soldiers, much of the region has remained largely unchanged, discouraging developers and road builders with its wild, rugged scenery and often harsh climate.

Outside Northumbria most people think of it as a cold, desolate land in all but the summer months, but that is a mistaken view. It is a place for all seasons, where frost and snow enhance the scene, and where the rare alpine flowers are reminiscent of Austria or Switzerland.

I have selected five journeys which I believe capture the mystery and drama of this enormous kingdom and it is for this reason that I have sadly neglected the great industrial towns which the same spirit pervades. It has been a fascinating experience composing this book, but it is not necessary for the reader to undertake these journeys all at one time other than in the imagination, which can be allowed to run free.

First is the romantic coastal route from Berwick-upon-Tweed to Warkworth, including a pilgrimage to the Holy Island of Lindisfarne – a journey of castles, kippers, seals and saints. This is followed by a journey through history and space in the captivating and breathless scenery of Kielder in the heart of Northumberland. The third journey is along Emperor Hadrian's Wall, the 'North West Frontier of Rome', with its fortresses wrapped like a necklace around the throat of Northumbria. Fourthly, a journey along the River Wear to the glorious City of Durham, 'the finest visual experience in the world', with its towering cathedral and castle dominating the ancient peninsula on which they stand. The final journey is along Teesdale, 'a natural laboratory of evolution of rare animals, birds and plants – relics of the ice age'. Pounding waterfalls and rare natural beauty are suffused with images of Dickens and Lewis Carroll, who both knew it well.

The illustrations have been chosen to evoke the spirit of this largely unspoilt ancient kingdom of Northern England – a mixture of ruggedness and romance, independence and isolation – the legacy of nature and the saints and sinners of the past.

These 'journeys' can be followed on the Ordnance Survey Landranger 1:50,000 maps and on the AA or Bartholomew Road Atlas.

CHAPTER ONE

Holy Island of Lindisfarne

NORTHUMBERLAND COAST

NORTHUMBERLAND COAST, CASTLES AND KIPPERS

BERWICK – HOLY ISLAND – BAMBURGH – CRASTER – WARKWORTH
(Distance 45 miles)

O The Bonny Fisher Lad

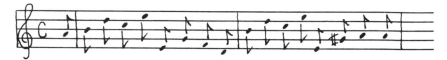

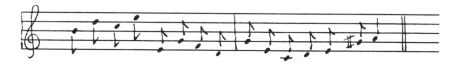

On Bamboroughshire's rocky shore,
Just as you enter Boumer Raw,
There lives the bonny fisher lad,
The fisher lad that bangs them a'.

O the bonny fisher lad,
That brings the fishes frae the sea,
O the bonny fisher lad,
The fisher lad gat had o' me.

Northumberland is known for its desolate moors, rugged Cheviot hills and sparkling rivers, but it deserves to be remembered most for its eighty miles of coastline, two-thirds of which has been designated an area of 'outstanding natural beauty'. It is one vast and fascinating nature reserve, rich in history, romantic folklore and wildlife.

Standing on a spectacular cliff with panoramic views, it's like surveying some long lost land inhabited only by colonies of sea birds and grey seals. Yet the remains of great castles, the evocative silhouettes of Dunstanburgh and Bamburgh, recall its wild and turbulent past.

What is it that makes the Northumberland coast so extraordinary? The infinite variety of landscape and scenery, some would say. But that is not the answer – the whole of the British Isles' coastline can boast that. Colour, adventure and history – add these to the list and you are nearer the mark. Tension, struggle and the blood of thousands – now the pulse quickens. But there is one last ingredient – the people; kind but tough, intelligent without being smart, dour but friendly, humorous yet not mocking.

This is a journey along the coast, and through history. Although more than forty miles long, the route is closely followed by the London to Edinburgh main railway line, so that it is possible to complete the journey in under twenty-five minutes on an InterCity 125 train – there is even a guide that you can buy to help you. However, at that speed you only get frustratingly brief and tantalising glimpses. It is a journey that warrants a more sedate pace to explore its strings of castles, beaches, islands and harbours.

We begin at Berwick-upon-Tweed. If Berwick were in Scotland and the River

N

Berwick-upon-Tweed

Holy Island (Lindisfarne)

Farne Islands

Bamburgh

Seahouses

NORTH SEA

Wooler

Embleton

Craster

A1

A697

The Cheviot

Boulmer

Alnwick

Alnmouth

Warkworth

R. Coquet

0 Miles 5

THE NORTHUMBERLAND COAST

Tweed the border, it would be more dramatic sweeping over the Royal Border Bridge by train or the Royal Tweed Bridge by car. Travellers would feel they had crossed a frontier and arrived. Instead, the actual border is marked by a sign in a field three miles north of the town – an anticlimax. Yet Berwick *feels* English, even if some think of it as Scottish, but it sees itself as a separate entity.

Though the A1 now by-passes Berwick, relieving it of the worst of the traffic, it still remains a lively place, with a cascade of narrow grey streets and Dutch-tiled roofs, all contained within the massive city walls. The bustle of the town centre contrasts sharply with the quiet of the surrounding streets, and exposed to the wind and any other elements the weather has to offer, walking along the walls is a totally different experience, with marvellous views along the coast. Here you feel surrounded by history.

Wandering around Berwick you can see some fine examples of the conservation of old buildings. This is a town which now *cares* about its buildings – a pleasant contrast to the last century, when the railway engineers demolished most of the castle to build the station.

On the river the swans are a traditional feature. Though decimated by oil pollution a few years ago they are now flourishing, as is the black economy – the poaching of salmon! The salmon are still very much a part of the life of the Tweed.

At the top of Marygate, the main street, is Scotsgate. It is hard to visualise now, but until a couple of years ago all the traffic on the A1 had to thread through this narrow gate. Climbing up the steps onto the walls and walking eastwards towards the coast you come to the Cumberland Bastion with its cannon. This gives a good impression of the scale and elaborate design of these fortifications. Further along there is a superb view of the sweep of the coast to the grey bumps of Holy Island,

Royal Border Bridge, Berwick

Bamburgh and the Farne Islands. Continuing your walk along the wall you soon come to Ravensdowne Barracks, the headquarters and museum of the King's Own Scottish Borderers, the regiment, incidentally, in which my grandfather served as Regimental Sergeant Major until his arm was shot off in action.

In more ancient times it was here in bloodstained Berwick that Edward I of England in 1295 began his 'hammering of the Scots' by attacking what was then Scotland's largest and richest port. The people fought until they died. Those not burnt to death were put to the sword and the blood of seven thousand men, women and children washed the cobbled streets, running like a river to colour the Tweed deep red. Bodies were not permitted to be buried, churches were taken as billets and stables for soldiers and horses.

The Scots twice recaptured the town during the hundred years that followed, but it was finally taken for England in 1482 by Richard, Duke of Gloucester, later King Richard III.

This blessed plot, this earth, this realm, this England . . .
This land of such dear souls, this dear, dear land!

(from 'Richard II')

The walker is brought back to the present by the ear-splitting crescendo of a Tornado jet as it swoops in low from the coast; a common occurrence in this area.

Move on to climb the Windmill Bastion next, stepping over the iron tracks and old gun-emplacements which look like some hopelessly engineered playground. Below *is* a children's playground, complete with climbing frame in the shape of a military tank. . . .

9

Though the walls continue southwards, for brevity one can turn down the side of the magazine house where you come face to face with two stone lions guarding what is imaginatively called the 'Lions House'. It is now three private flats and a good example of the sensitive conservation in Berwick over the past decade. Follow the path to Ravensdowne by Browns Hotel, on past the Post Office to the junction of Marygate and Hyde Hill under the shadow of the Town House where, on the ground floor, which once contained lock-up cells, the Exchange and the Buttermarket, there is a very informative map and potted history of Berwick.

You don't have to be interested in bridges to appreciate the Royal Border Bridge, a railway viaduct designed by Robert Stephenson and opened by Queen Victoria in 1850. It is 2152 feet long and 126 feet high and is supported on twenty-eight arches built on a sweeping curve. This is in sharp contrast to the Royal Tweed Bridge, opened in 1928 by the then Prince of Wales – useful but ugly.

The old Berwick Bridge, the earlier road bridge, is the fifth known to have been built on the same site. The James VI bridge, as it is sometimes called, is a warm stone-arched bridge with 15 foot spans, and is 1200 feet long. It was built between 1609 and 1634 as a direct result of the king having been frightened to death on the rickety wooden bridge it replaced. The king, so it is said, became so terrified as he rode across that he threw himself off his horse into the river and had to be dragged out. (James VI of Scotland became James I of England).

Of Berwick Castle, on which the railway station stands, little remains, but it was here that Isabella, sister of the Earl of Fife, was suspended in a cage for four years as punishment for placing the crown on Robert the Bruce's head!

As we leave Berwick and its troubled past and promising future, what are we to make of the descriptive lines ascribed to Robert Burns? –

A bridge without a middle arch,
A church without a steeple,
A midden heap in every street
And damned conceited people.

Not much!

Back in the car drive via Bridge End and Berwick Bridge, across the river into Tweedmouth. After Berwick, Tweedmouth has the feeling of the Cinderella partner, hosting the Tweed's industrial waterfront with its small harbour. Without being unkind, the best aspect is that across the river to Berwick.

Turn left on to Spittal Promenade – still a fine view across the river, with sea birds on the mud flats at low tide. Turn right at the crossroads past the church into Albert Road until you reach the level-crossing over the main line. Here one has to wait for the lady crossing-keeper to open the gates – and on Friday mornings, to do her shopping at the mobile shop as well!

Before reaching the A1 there is a good view of the Cheviots. Turn left on to the main road and head south along what is a fast, busy stretch. Do not stop at Haggerston Castle – only the tower remains, surrounded by a caravan park and lay-by. Less than two miles on, at the Plough Hotel, turn left for Beal and Holy Island.

Before embarking on this part of the journey it is essential to check the tide times carefully to ensure that you can cross the causeway and get back safely. There are tidetables where you turn off the A1, or you can telephone the AA/RAC. It is vital that you check the times accurately, for the tide rises very rapidly and it is not unusual for visitors to become stranded. Pass through the

St Aidan and Holy Island

tiny village of Beal and drop down to the causeway. Note the tall refuge tower in the middle for those who get caught by the tide!

I have been to the Holy Island of Lindisfarne many times and enjoyed it more each time, but I cannot be sure why. A pilgrimage to Lindisfarne is more than a journey of discovery, but it would be extravagant to claim that it is a mystical experience. Its historical and religious connections, though real, exist without the symbolism of a religious presence such as a monastery. Yet it was here, in the very cradle of this country's Christianity, that a monastery was founded by St. Aidan in 635 AD. It nurtured nine saints and sixteen bishops, the greatest of whom was St. Cuthbert, who was originally buried here, but later re-buried behind the altar in Durham Cathedral following the Viking invasion.

However, in our secular age scant religious attention is paid to this, the most holy place in England. Some interest was aroused to celebrate St. Cuthbert's 1300th anniversary in 1987, but no religious community now exists here other than the local church and a retreat for young people.

If there is a religious experience to be had, I find it on the southern side, at St. Cuthbert's Isle on Hobthrush, a grass-covered basaltic rock accessible only at low tide. Here are the remains of the saint's own chapel where he kept a lamp aglow during the night to guide the fishermen back into harbour, and where he made his rosaries. There is a stone cross where the altar once stood. Here at night:–

> *St. Cuthbert sits, and toils to frame*
> *The sea-born beads that bear his name:*
> *Such tales had Whitby's fishers told,*
> *And said they might his shape behold,*

13

And here his anvil sound;
A deadened clang – a huge dim form,
Seen but, and heard, when gathering storm
And night were closing round.

Holy Island was at the heart of the cruel battles between the English and the Scots. Four hundred years ago ten line-of-battle English warships were anchored in the harbour with thousands of soldiers thirsting for blood. But however you look at this historical and religious paradox, the island is an attractive place in its own right. Its main features, such as the castle, priory, St. Aidan's statue and the harbour, could have been arranged by a skilled painter or photographer, and Nature too has provided a sanctuary to delight the eye.

The two elements of climate which have the greatest effect on plants and animals are temperature and rainfall. Cool and dry, close to the Arctic air and furthest from the warm westerlies of the Atlantic, many of the plants that can be seen here are those which owe their origins to Scandinavia; the elegant, pink twinflower being one of these. Salt and wind, inhibiting the growth of trees and shrubs, produces grotesque shapes due to the death of the buds on the windward side. Blackthorn is the tallest shrub, but there are many plants which do survive, nestling in rocks and nourished by the rotting remains blown by the wind. The more striking shrubs seen are the thrift, spring squill, sea campion and wild thyme. The rock samphire was made famous in *King Lear*:–

Half-way down the cliffs hangs one that gathers
Samphire, a dreadful trade.

Northumberland Coast

A dreadful trade, but a beautiful flower, multi-headed and pale yellow.

On the shores the tufted sand-dunes are dazzling white in the sunshine, adorned with fleshy varieties of plants such as the sea rocket and sea spurge. Exposed to salt spray, the sea bindweed creeps along the sand, pushing out its white bell-like morning glory flowers and shining leaves, and here and there the butterflies are active – the small copper and common blue. Birds swoop down to the sea and on to the shore. The famous eider ducks breed here, large gulleries and turneries vie with the guillemots and kittiwakes for space, intent on depriving the eight-thousand-strong colony of grey seals on the Farne Islands of their meal – the vast armada of salmon which gathers for its annual journey up the Tweed to the hills.

The early history of Holy Island is clear and precise, thanks to the writings of the Venerable Bede in the seventh century. Prior to this we only have pieces of flint and spearheads dating back to 10,000 BC to recall the distant past. Bede tells us that it was King Oswald of Northumbria who demanded that his monasteries send someone to convert his kingdom to Christianity. The monks on Iona, off the west coast of Scotland, sent Irish born St. Aidan to establish a community on Lindisfarne in 635 AD. When Aidan died, Cuthbert, a shepherd, took his place.

The island's name comes from the small stream called 'Lindis' and 'farne' meaning retreat. Later it took the name Insula Sacra, or Holy Island, when a Benedictine monastry was established in 1082 AD. The priory is now a graceful ruin.

One of the finest surviving works of art in England came from Holy Island – a beautifully illuminated manuscript, the Lindisfarne Gospels, which is now preserved and on display in the British Museum. It is a masterpiece of fantastic intricacy, written on the skins of over a thousand calves in 700 AD, and is the

earliest surviving English version of the four Gospels. Simeon of Durham narrates the story of the fate that nearly overtook the precious document in 870 AD as the monks were fleeing for their lives and their ship was stricken by a storm:–

In this storm while the ship was lying over on her side, a copy of the Gospels, adorned with gold and precious stones, fell overboard and sank into the depths of the sea. . .

Amidst their lamentations their pious patron came to their aid; for appearing in a vision to one of them, Hunred by name, he bade them seek at low-tide for the manuscript which had fallen from the ship into the midst of the waves. . .

Accordingly they go to the sea and find that it had retired much further than it was accustomed; and after walking three miles or more they find the sacred manuscript of the Gospels itself, exhibiting all its outer splendour of jewels and gold and all the beauty of its pages and writing within, as though it had never been touched by water.

The castle is both a disappointment and a delight. A disappointment in that one might expect an emphasis on fortification and armoury; a delight because one can see how a decaying castle was taken by a relatively modern architect, Sir Edwin Lutyens, and transformed into a home in which to live with such painstaking attention to detail. Visit the house, where the rooms, like so many Dutch interiors, have an austere background decorated with English oak furniture, paintings and brasswork. The vaulted kitchens contain the finest copperware, such as fish kettles, pots and pans. The sturdy pink columns are reminiscent of Durham Cathedral; a nautical air is created by a model of a three-masted ship hanging from the ceiling in the Ship Room and many fine pieces of pottery bearing the cipher of the Royal Yacht. The great event in the more recent life of the castle was the visit in 1908 of the Prince and Princess of

Wales. In the west bedroom there is an inscription on the bed beneath a carved bird:–

ANN MARIE ENGLEBOTT ERBJIS OM AIJ EDERFALS

Its meaning remains a complete mystery.

The whole castle, now owned by the National Trust, is a remarkable tribute to a great architect – masterly, romantic and the outstanding feature of this lovely island.

Because all the visitors flock to the village, priory, harbour and castle, the links along the north of the island provide a beautiful and quiet backwater for a walk. At one time the island was literally a rabbit warren, or at least the sandy parts and old limestone quarry at the Snook, nearest to the coast. There are over three hundred recorded species of birds, the most famous of which are the eiders, known locally as 'Cuthbert's chicks'. The fulmar breeds on the island along with wigeons, kittiwakes, guillemots, puffins and shags. The greylag geese are regular visitors – as many as twelve hundred at a time. Roe deer and foxes can be seen on the prowl in winter.

If you have to take a souvenir from Holy Island, you are encouraged to buy a bottle of Lindisfarne Mead or any one of a number of commodities which are laced with it, such as fudge. A paradox perhaps, that a place with such ascetic connotations should actively market as a souvenir . . . an aphrodisiac!

A striking feature of the island is the use of large upturned boats as sheds, if not dwellings. I had only previously seen such usage in BBC TV's production of *David Copperfield*, but never in reality. I don't know why they're such a feature here, but it's a fascinating sight, these upturned clinker hulls, complete with windows and doors. Beyond the castle are three perfectly preserved examples, but there are many more.

Fishing has always played a part in the life of the island, but never more so than in the nineteenth century when most of the population was employed in the industry and the streets were piled high with stinking fish, lines, shells and rubbish. Twenty boats were used to catch herring, whiting, crab, lobster, cod, salmon, mussells and winkles. Two fishwives, who used to sell their wares carried on donkeys, have been committed to verse – Smelly Bessie and Pallid Sally.

> *Twas in that place called Holy Isle*
> *Two damsels dressed in fishwife style*
> *Each with a cud their way would wend*
> *Far up the country their fish to vend*
> *One was Sall – the other Bess*
> *The fish they hawked were seldom fresh*
> *But fresh or stale they aye got trade,*
> *By making dupes a living made.*
> *Sall was long and lean and lank*
> *Her shape was like a six foot plank*
> *Her mate, fat Bess, as her name implies*
> *Was a mass of flesh of enormous size.*

Another occupation of the folk on Lindisfarne was the salvaging of shipwrecks. Not for nothing is the tale told of the fisherman's prayer, 'Lord send us a good wreck.'

19

Bamburgh Castle

The local dialect only serves to emphasise that this is an island. Sitting in one of the pubs (where allegedly the licensing hours vary directly with the tidetables!) the conversation between the local fishermen is almost totally unintelligible.

Retrace your steps to the A1 and continue your journey southwards for a few miles until you reach a left turn marked Elwick and Easington Grange. Again, cross the main line by the level-crossing and you find yourself driving through a large farm.

If you wish to enjoy an optional diversion, turn left just beyond Elwick, across the links leading to Ross Back sands, a fine sweep of glorious sand four miles in length. Otherwise, continue along flat, rich farmland to Warren Mill. Half-left across the fields is Budle Bay, a nature reserve, in the news recently when some men were prosecuted for digging up bait worms.

The road now climbs to give a splendid long view back to Holy Island, but if you stop, don't let your eyes drop or the scene is spoilt by the pile of old washing machines and other scrap dumped from the lay-by – and this is in a National Nature Reserve!

Turning inland you have a few moments' respite from this overwhelming scenery before the crest of the hill when . . . there it is, straight in front of you – Bamburgh Castle, totally dominating the view, broadside on. The castle is so prominent as to be almost arrogant, that is until you draw nearer, when it becomes at first incredible, then fascinating and friendly. Film-makers love it. The scenes in *Becket* were shot here, and the arrival of Richard Burton and Elizabeth Taylor brought the village to a standstill. Ken Russell also made *The Devils* here.

You come first to the ancient church of St. Aidan where a sign tells you that people have worshipped here since 635 AD. The saint himself not only founded the church and used it as his home, but also died here in a tent outside.

The existing church is *only* eight hundred years old and there are numerous memorials to Northumbrian saints and heroines. One startling feature is the low side-window where people stricken by the plague could receive communion without entering the church. There is also an effigy of Grace Darling, and a monument to her in the churchyard. Unfortunately, the elaborate Victorian superstructure is rather overdone. However, it is visible to sailors at sea, its size reflecting the way this local girl captured the imagination of the people.

Grace was born in 1815, in a cottage next to the museum opposite the church. She was the daughter of the Farne Islands lighthouse-keeper, William. When she was ten, the family moved to the new Longstone lighthouse erected on the Farne Islands, and lived there until the disaster of 7 September 1838, when the luxury liner the S.S. *Forfarshire* struck a rock in a raging storm. Forty-three passengers were drowned but Grace, who spotted the wreck first, and her father braved the treacherous seas in their coble rowing boat to save eight men and a woman.

Having survived the perils of that night, this pale, shy, twenty-two-year-old girl, racked with consumption, died four years later in the house in Bamburgh which later became the Post Office. Those four years, however, were amazing. Her heroism triggered a surge of emotion through the land. She was inundated with offers of marriage, invitations and gifts. She was even invited to appear in London at the Adelphi Theatre, being offered £10 a week to row her boat across the stage twice nightly!

The museum contains her coble, pictures, documents, locks of hair and other relics. 'Is there in the whole field of history, or of fiction, even one instance of female heroism to compare for one moment with this?' So asked a *Times* leader. And even the great Wordsworth waxed lyrical:–

Bamburgh

And through the sea's tremendous trough
The father and the girl rode off . . .

The Longstone lighthouse still operates, though now with radar, and was the target of German bombers in 1941 when it was partially destroyed.

The King of Northumbria, Ethelfrith (593–616 AD) married Queen Bebba and as a wedding present he re-named the fortress Bebbanburgh (Bebba's town). York was the capital, but Bebbanburgh, or Bamburgh as it later became, remained the royal residence until it fell into disuse, eventually to be pillaged and sacked by the Danes. Its famous relics, the uncorrupted head and hand of St. Oswald, were stolen at this time.

Eventually, with various sieges involving the Scots and the Wars of the Roses to its credit, Bamburgh languished in ruins until 1704 when its fortunes were restored. It was bought by the Bishop of Durham, Lord Crewe, who turned it into a girls' school. It was finally acquired and restored by Lord Armstrong – though not without criticism from the conservationists who condemned the unthinking enthusiasm of one of the leading engineers, whose name later became associated with Vickers in Newcastle.

Part of the castle has now been leased off as flats, but it is still worth walking round the massive walls, bailey and keep, and visiting the King's Hall hung with paintings and rich tapestries. The armoury has a large collection of weapons, some on loan from the Tower of London, but the castle does not now reflect its former glory, and perhaps those long views as you approach and leave are the best remembered part of it.

Bamburgh village, despite its popularity, its Georgian cottages, tea rooms and inn enclosing the triangular green which narrows as it nears the castle, remains unspoilt.

Seahouses

From which ever way you enter or leave Bamburgh there are glorious views of the sea, the coast and the Cheviots. We follow the road to the south, the B1340, which runs along the foot of the castle rock and close by the shore among the sand dunes towards Seahouses.

Before continuing it is interesting to note that geologists are fascinated by what is known as the Great Whin Sill – a wide flat sheet of toughened magna which starts in North Yorkshire and travels northwards, outcropping at Hadrian's Wall, Craster, Bamburgh and the Farne Islands. On the beaches you will find white limestone, yellow sandstone, coal and magna, all about three hundred million years old. *And* you may find coral in the limestone – a rare occurrence reflecting the fact that this coast was at one time situated in the southern tropics! What with the Whin Sill and the coral, half the tourists are budding geologists, drawn to this great wonder of Europe to gaze and to hammer away!

Seahouses is the sailing point for the Farne Islands, which lie two to five miles off shore and they can be clearly seen from here. The attraction of these fifteen or so islands is totally different from that of Holy Island. There seems little danger (apart from the tide) in getting to Holy Island, but the Farnes strike fear in the visitor (perhaps fuelled by the legend of Grace Darling) and to confirm it, they have *two* lighthouses.

If you love sea birds, seals, salmon and solitude, go there. But go in one of the open, low-sided fishing boats which will add to the excitement, rather than the 'posh' steamer registered in Poole. After all, it's not a pleasure trip, is it?

There are two main aspects to Seahouses. Firstly it is a working village, and second it proliferates fish-and-chip shops and amusement arcades. *But* the fish and chips are excellent and the planners obviously like to keep the tourists in Seahouses on the 'honey pot' principle. If you do take a trip to the Farne Islands it is as well to remember that the crossing can be quite rough, so have your fish-and-chips after you return! You will have a ravenous appetite and a more lasting appreciation of their flavour.

The working aspect of Seahouses is on view in the harbour, which is usually full of fishing boats, and the quays are piled high with lobster pots, fish-boxes and nets, while the eiders can be seen swimming in the harbour.

Now press on. From the harbour, drive up the main street to the roundabout and turn left for Beadnell, about two miles along the road. Unlike Seahouses, Beadnell has the feeling of definitely *not* being a working place, but more a relaxing holiday haven. The buildings are painted white, and the more affluent Tynesiders are much in evidence with their dinghies.

North of Beadnell harbour the sand has given way to rocks and shingle but immediately to the south is a fine curve of beach with yet another castle on a rocky promontory of the Great Whin Sill – Dunstanburgh.

To remind you that Beadnell was once a real working place, on the quayside are some beautiful old lime kilns in the care of the National Trust, the notice on them telling you that:–

In 1798 it was agreed that Richard Pringle should build a lime kiln measuring twenty-four feet in height:– the kiln to provide 1000 cartloads of lime each year to be exported by sea to ports in England and Scotland.

From the harbour, retrace your steps to the main road and rejoin the B1340 to Swinhoe. At Swinhoe turn left at the crossroads and follow the signs for Embleton.

Embleton is a sizeable village with a fortified vicarage. At the end of the main street the road to Craster and Howick sweeps to the right. A few hundred yards along is a track to the left which leads to the golf course, where you can see the magnificent sight of Dunstanburgh Castle, perched on its dolomite cliff. The huge bastions still guard this broken pile which covers eleven acres. With the northern flank protected by the cliff, the original keep stood five storeys high. But why so massive, and why build a castle here at all? There's no settlement, no harbour, no river. Was it someone's folly? It is supposed to have been a tribal meeting place at one time, but in profile, especially when seen from the train, it puts you in mind of a stranded oil tanker. It was built in the fourteenth century by Thomas of Lancaster and the gatehouse was later enlarged to form a keep by John o'Gaunt during the Wars of the Roses. Henry VI's fighting queen, Margaret, captured the place, but then lost it again in 1464 and it has now lain in ruins for four hundred years. It may have its ghosts, but it has certainly become the haunt of artists, including Turner, who painted the castle many times.

Along this stretch of coast there are concrete pillboxes and fortifications which were built to meet the expected German invasion in the Second World War. With its long deserted beaches and sea front this is a natural place for covert activities, as we shall see when we reach Boulmer.

From here you can walk to Craster along the coastal path – if you can persuade someone to drive round there to pick you up. If a walk does not appeal, it is better to retrace your steps to the lane and follow the signpost for Craster along the unclassified road.

At Craster leave your car in the car park before going down to the harbour where a few fishing boats can be seen. The large concrete structure on the end of the harbour wall once accommodated machinery for loading locally quarried stone into coastal ships. Many of London's kerb stones are made from Craster whinstone. The fishing boats are cobles, dragged up the shingle beach on log rollers. Knowledgeable writers make much of the association of cobles with the Farne Islands, but to my uninformed eye the boats sailing there are not cobles but traditional English and Scottish fishing boats. The coble, with its distinctive shape and twin keel, exposed when out of water, is more elegant and much safer in rough waters. But whatever the details of construction, it plays a significant part in the life of the Northumbrian coast as far down as Whitby, and that other old centre of smuggling operations, Robin Hood's Bay. The coble is now motorised, of course, though some masts can still be seen.

Up the hill on the south side of the harbour is the place Craster is famous for – the kipper house, or kippery. It is not so long ago that British Rail used to serve fresh Craster kippers for breakfast on the 'Newcastle Executive', but you may have to settle for less now. When kippers are being cured here the smell is wonderful – if you like the smell of kippers, that is. The humble herring, alas too few of them now due to modern fishing methods, is first split, salted and smoked, and then hung in rows over a low fire sprinkled with oak chips and sawdust. Most kippers you buy have not been cured in this way; but once you've tasted a Craster smoke-cured kipper you'll know the difference.

If the smell of kippers is not to your liking, Craster offers an excellent alternative attraction – a walk which you ought to take whether you need to escape from the kippers or not. This is the walk par excellence of this journey.

From the north end of the village there is a beautiful cliff-top path back to Dunstanburgh castle a mile away. The turf springs beneath your feet, the sea splashes up on the rocks and the eiders bob up and down in the swell. Only a short walk, yet all the time you are conscious of every aspect of this land of

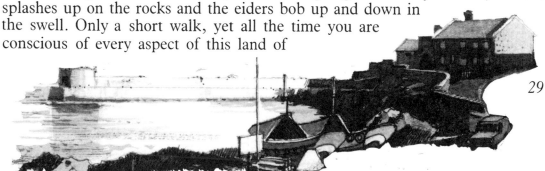

29

Northumbria. Castle, coast, countryside, wildlife, sea and sand. A pleasant moment to take it all in, in one gulp.

Time to go. Take the southern road to Howick through rich farmland and then rejoin the B1339, following the signs to Longhoughton, noted for its RAF radar and helicopter stations. Turn left after the village, following the sign 'RAF Boulmer'. The entrance to the station is marked by a Lightning aircraft – strange, since the station only possesses two Sea King helicopters. They provide emergency cover for the coast and as far west as Cumbria, where I've watched them in action, picking an injured climber off the misty peak of Glaramara.

Boulmer village, just past the RAF station, is potentially attractive though it does its best not to be, looking a bit 'tatty'. More cobles and lobster pots and although no harbour, there is a haven sheltered by the rocks. The old lifeboat house looks run-down, but it does accommodate a volunteer rescue boat service.

Boulmer was once the smuggling centre of Northumbria and home of the infamous Isaac Addison, keeper of the Fishing Boat Inn. 'Isaac the Smuggler', as he was called a hundred years ago, was a tall, handsome man who used to entertain the Duke of Northumberland in his bar parlour to lend it an air of respectability. But unfortunately for him his nefarious operations were brought to a sudden end, as the story in the *Newcastle Magazine* of 1872 relates:–

Isaac owned a lugger, which he called the *Ides*. He had twenty-four hands on board, and a large and lucrative trade he did for a time. But one evening, when near Boulmer harbour, it was fired at by a government cutter. The smugglers retaliated, and a desperate fight ensued. The scene of combat extended from Boulmer to Robin Hood's Bay. Night was setting in on the combatants, and the smugglers began to think they were fighting a losing game. They had shot two of the king's men, but one of their own crew was killed, and another's leg was broken. Thinking there was no hope of victory, they therefore lowered their boat during the darkness, and after sinking the *Ides*, rowed manfully for home. They got to Boulmer far ahead of the royal cutter, and managed to land their dead and wounded; and, as two eye-witnesses informed me, they split up their boat and stowed it into a hole in a cottage, now occupied by Ann Richardson, next to the Fishing Boat Inn. The crew, with the exception of Isaac, fled away inland. The noted smuggler was soon apprehended. Sentence of death for shooting at the king's men now hung over him. The day of trial came, and with it the acquittal of Addison – simply, however, because the royal cutter had not hoisted its colours before firing on the smugglers. This happened about fifty years ago, and was the last of the smuggling at Boulmer.

With its radar scanners, Boulmer is part of the NATO early warning network. Covert operations seem somehow to suit its character.

Now follow the coastal road to Alnmouth, to an elevated position where you can see the lower reaches of the River Aln enclosing low-lying meadows. From this vantage point the road drops down into Alnmouth.

Seen from a distance (usually from the train) I always think Alnmouth looks a wonderfully sleepy little village – and driving into it does little to change that feeling, for it has become a dormitory town for Newcastle commuters. At the roundabout go straight on and down the main street; then at the bottom you can either turn left to the beach car park or follow the road to a dead end. From the latter you have a grand view over the mouth of the Aln down to Amble and Coquet Island. Here again are many World War II tank traps and pillboxes still visible among the sand dunes. It was once a good harbour for ships and in 1779 even merited the attention of the infamous pirate, Paul Jones, who bombarded the port. Paul Jones was, in fact, the commander of an American ship *The Ranger* which was operating in a joint action with the French. It's known that one cannon ball missed the church and fell in a field. There is, after all, reason to retain the trappings of modern warfare!

Now on the 'home straight' of our journey, follow the A1068 which runs alongside the railway till it veers away towards Warkworth. The main road now crosses the River Coquet on a modern bridge which spans the river close to the medieval stone bridge with its very unusual fortified toll house at the south end.

Warkworth is an exciting small town, picturesquely placed at the mouth of the Coquet, with marvellous views over the loop of the river to the sea and Coquet Island with its lighthouse. It certainly played a key role in many battles from Saxon times onwards. The castle has been re-built in the past and the present ruins date from the fourteenth century. It's a good castle to look round, with enough remaining to get the atmosphere of the spaces and the feel of the stonework. Some may remember Anneka Rice's runabout in TV's *Treasure Hunt*, trying to find the 'fireplace in the Lantern'.

The first castle here was built in 1140 by Henry, the son of David I, King of Scotland. Two hundred years later, in 1332, it was given to Lord Percy of Alnwick by King Edward II. Edward I stayed here, as did King John, but William the Lion, in 1173:–

did not deigne to stop there, for weak was the castle, the wall and the trench.

The first Earl of Northumberland, a Percy, lived at Warkworth and had a son called Harry Hotspur, who became a hero of the battle of Otterburn and had his name enshrined in the ballad of that name. Harry Hotspur was killed in battle far from home in Shrewsbury, whereupon Henry IV marched north and captured Warkworth. A number of the scenes in Shakespeare's *Henry IV* are set in Warkworth.

32

Warkworth

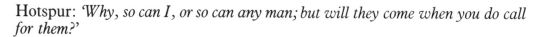

'I am not yet of Percy's mind, the Hotspur of the North; he that kills me some six or seven dozen of Scots at a breakfast, washes his hands, and says to his wife, "Fie upon this quiet life! I want work".'

(Part 1, Act 2, Scene 4)

★ ★ ★ ★ ★

Glendower: *'I can call spirits from the vasty deep.'*

Hotspur: *'Why, so can I, or so can any man; but will they come when you do call for them?'*

(Part 1, Act 3, Scene 1)

Turner, of course, painted the castle, the Scots destroyed it, the Danes destroyed it too, villagers were massacred in it, boiling lead was poured from the keep on to the heads of invaders, and treason was plotted here. Yet close by is a Norman church of rare beauty and tranquility which is worth investigation in its own right.

The town itself has everything a small town should have – good hotels, pubs, restaurants with high quality food, neat, tidy houses, all contained within the loop of the river. And the castle on its huge mound dominates the scene, forming a spectacular viewing platform for the coast and countryside.

There is no better place to end our first journey of exploration, with the anticipation of Alnwick and Hexham to follow.

34

CHAPTER TWO

Kielder Water

KIELDER WATER

KIELDER WATER AND THE BORDER FORESTS

ALNWICK – ROTHBURY – OTTERBURN – KIELDER – HEXHAM
(Distance 90 miles)

The Hexhamshire Lass

Hey for the buff and the blue,
Hey for the cap and the feather,
Hey for the bonny lass true,
That lives in Hexhamshire.

This journey encounters large open spaces, which are in sharp contrast to small settlements. Despite being swollen by Newcastle commuters, Alnwick and Hexham still only have populations of under ten thousand. Rothbury has less than two thousand. Yet Kielder Forest covers 175,000 acres, Kielder Water 2,648 acres, and at Otterburn the biggest military range in Europe occupies 55,000 acres.

The region's greatest treasure is its history, richly told in stories and ballads. Prehistoric man settled here, the Romans buried their dead here, and the English and Scots fought their battles over this ground – Otterburn stands alongside Flodden, as the bloodiest and most heroic. Violence, the gibbet and whisky smuggling all flourished well into the eighteenth century.

You don't have to be a Barbour-coated, green-wellied, outdoor-type to find a deer, an otter or your favourite wild flowers. You can drive or walk unhindered through hundreds of acres of new and ancient woodlands, vast sweeps of moorland, and past secret burns that tumble through this hauntingly beautiful piece of Northumbria which brushes Scotland's borders, and see them all. Winter here is an incredible and romantic sight, but remember that the A68, the Roman road, is always the first route to Scotland to become blocked by snow.

Early Man

They inhabit wild and waterless mountains and desolate and marshy plains, having no walls nor cities nor tilled land, but living off flocks and wild animals and some fruits. They live in tents, naked and unshod, holding their women in common and rearing their offspring together. Such is the island of Brittania and such its inhabitants, at least of the hostile part of it.

(Cassius Dio, AD 200)

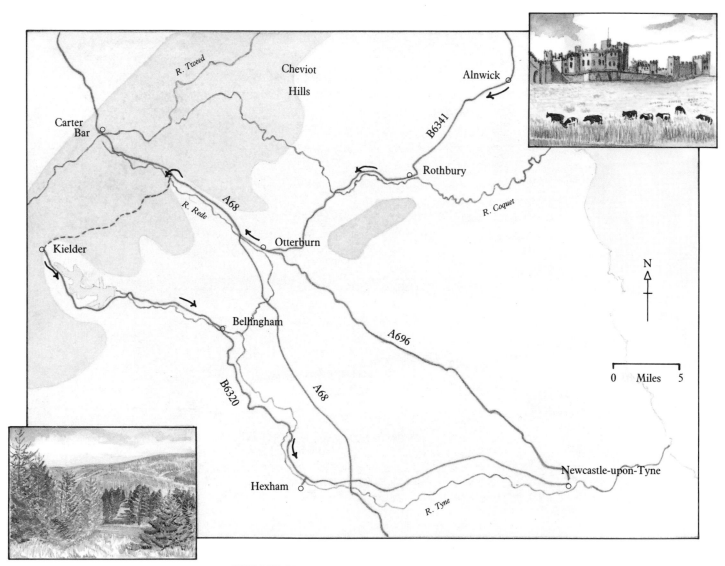

R. Tweed

Cheviot
Hills

Alnwick

Carter
Bar

B6341

Rothbury

A68

R. Rede

R. Coquet

Kielder

Otterburn

Bellingham

A696

B6320

A68

N

0 Miles 5

Hexham

Newcastle-upon-Tyne

R. Tyne

KIELDER WATER AND THE BORDER FORESTS

You really need more than one day to explore, but it can still be enjoyed in a day, and if you haven't the time to go there, then sit back and imagine it all as we journey from Alnwick to Hexham, away from the main routes except for a short distance on the A68.

If you commence up the hill just north of Alnwick (pronounced 'Annick'), beyond the Lion Bridge on the old A1, you can get a good impression of the huge scale of Alnwick Castle which isn't possible from within the town. This was the view Turner chose for his famous moonlit painting. The feature of the Lion Bridge, designed by Robert and John Adam, is the lion with its 'Ramrod-tail'. The River Aln below is unimpressive by comparison, being covered with weeds of the sort that make it look like a rhubarb farm for Titans. The castle gatehouse is just up the short steep hill from the bridge.

The castle *is* the reason for Alnwick. Its origins in 1309 are tied to the Percy family who bought the land from the Bishop of Durham. The history of the Border country parallels the history of the Percys who came over with William the Conqueror from Normandy. In the valleys of the Rede and Tyne, the Percys' word was law – not the King's. They were survivors, who clung to their lands and tithes despite various descendants being killed in battle, executed and even occasionally running out of heirs. Yet they always found an heiress to carry them forward so, bending with the winds of change, they ran out winners in the end. Today Alnwick Castle remains the seat of the Percy family, the Earl and Duke of Northumberland.

The castle was used in 1650 by Cromwell to house some 6,000 Scottish prisoners, most of whom died of starvation and exposure, but that at least gives some idea of its size. It now consists of a central keep on a landscaped mound, surrounded by walls and turrets in a superb yet peaceful, pastoral setting. A

Alnwick Castle

good deal of Italian decoration is evidence of former glory. The Abbot's Tower houses the museum of the Royal Northumberland Fusiliers, with records of the American War of Independence and the Indian Mutiny.

In the dining room you can see a display which includes the uniform worn by Colonel the Hon. Henry Percy when he brought the first news of Waterloo to London. That is historically incorrect, of course, since the first news was carried to London by runners, fast ships and racing pigeons belonging to Nathan Rothschild, the financial genius. He reported the unexpected defeat of Napoleon direct to the Prime Minister long before the Hon. Henry arrived. His brother-in-law, Sir Moses Montefiore, went at the same time to the Stock Exchange with orders to buy, buy, buy! Sir Moses (my own great grandfather, according to my mother) made a substantial profit for Nathan and himself. In London they fought their battles with money. Here in the Borders they fought with blood.

The People

The people of this country hath had one barbarous custom amongst them; if any two be displeased, they expect no law, but bang it out bravely, one and his kindred against the other, and his; they will subject themselves to no justice, but in an inhumane and barbarous manner, fight and kill one another; they run together in clangs (as they terme it) or names.

This fighting they call their feides, or deadly feides, a word so barbarous, that I cannot express it in any other tongue.

(William Gray, 1649)

If you have time and like castles then linger here, otherwise pass by into Narrowgate, where on the left you will see Ye Olde Cross, a whitewashed pub with a bow-fronted Georgian window showing its famous 'dirty bottles'. A notice explains:–

> These bottles have been here for over 150 years. Whilst putting them here, the man collapsed and died. It was said that if anyone tried to move them they would share the same fate. They have never been moved since.

Yet I know of someone in Durham who claims that in his mis-spent youth he broke a pane of glass one dark night and stole a bottle . . . !

As Narrowgate becomes Bondgate you come to the centre of busy Alnwick. There are plenty of shops and a liberal sprinkling of hostelries such as the George and the Black Swan. It is pleasing to note that a modern supermarket has been built of stone that blends in well with the old buildings. There are plenty of Victorian-built banks and building societies reflecting the prosperity of the town.

The street widens out into a cobbled area until the luxurious White Swan Hotel is reached. Going through the archway of this old coaching house it is disappointing to find that the medieval buildings have been replaced by mediocre modern ones, and more cars.

Now move on to the Hotspur Tower – wrongly named, for it had nothing to do with Harry Hotspur, but no matter, it dominates everything with its solid triumphal arch of stone. It is difficult to imagine now, but within memory *all* the traffic between London and Edinburgh passed through this arch. This 'no nonsense' fortification bears little decoration apart from the inevitable Percy lion, but it is a vital part of the townscape. The tower marks the point of the town where the Council seems to have ceased to exercise its powers over planning consent. Beyond this there are only crude shop fronts and signs. Even the

Tenantry Column, Alnwick

Hotspur Tower itself has no less than ten road signs fixed to its south side. As for the large estate agent's on the ground floor of the old Playhouse cinema . . . !

Bondgate Without leads to the War Memorial and the Tenantry Column, the latter being eighty-three feet high and topped by the Percy lion. It is known as the Farmers' Folly, because after his tenants erected it in 1816 as a mark of gratitude for their low rents the Duke, impressed by their largesse, promptly increased them. 'Esperance en Dieu' is the inscription!

Opposite the Tenantry Column is the old railway station (is the lion watching for the next train to come?). This station, much grander than necessary, was designed to impress the Duke's important vistors, including royalty. It is now a 'cash and carry' warehouse.

In the market place, look out for Northumberland Hall and the Shambles. Then back to the car and find the B6341 road to Rothbury which climbs steeply out of Alnwick to the open moor, where the Royal Signals have built a radar screen at Brizlee Wood.

Within three or four miles of leaving Alnwick you already have a feeling of being in a remote area as you travel along a straight road with the Cheviot Hills visible to the north west. The road twists and turns by Corby's Crags perched on the hillside, while close to the road, below and to the right, what remains of the former Alnwick to Coldstream railway line can be seen. Edlingham viaduct, castle and church are on the right, and a diversion into the village (pronounced Edlin-jum) to see the Norman fortress is well worth the trouble. The rectory was the scene of an armed robbery two centuries ago. The judge, who had been born in the same house, sentenced two Alnwick poachers to life imprisonment. However, after ten years the men were pardoned when others confessed to the crime and as a result the English Court of Criminal Appeal was set up, but by

Cragside Hall

that time was of little comfort to the poachers.

Rich farmland here gives way to moorland and gorse and you may spot such colourful birds as the siskin, the redpoll, and even that majestic creature the emperor moth. The road crosses the A697 and climbs again until the crags of the Simonside Hills are visible in the distance.

As you enter Rothbury Forest the road turns and drops steeply. About a quarter of a mile into the forest there is a turning left to Cragside. It would be a crime to pass this extraordinary mansion, not just because of the house itself but also for the park, both now happily in the care of the National Trust. The drive round the park takes you past Tumbleton Lake, the stables, and dramatically through the house. To appreciate the splendour of the gardens, visit Cragside in June to see the masses and masses of rhododendrons. There are shops and picnic stops at places such as Black Burn Lake and Nelly's Moss Lake.

Lord Armstrong (remember Bamburgh Castle?), lawyer and engineer, built this as a place to relax in, but everything about the inside of the house is overbearingly formal without a hint of relaxation. 'Wagnerian', as it was once described. His architect, Norman Shaw, is renowned for building Scotland Yard in London. Perhaps he had this in mind at the time. Some liked it, though:–

And on yon brown and rocky hill
See princely Cragside lies,
Where boundless wealth and perfect taste
Have made a paradise.

Well, the money came from engineering and the armaments industry but, as Lord Armstrong told the County Council:–

I owe much to this district and it owes much to me, so there are mutual claims between you as inhabitants and myself.

What *is* interesting though is that this was the first private house in the land to be fitted with electric light. Devised by Lord Armstrong and his friend, Joseph Swan of Swan's Electric Lamps, the brook was dammed to provide hydro-electric power through a generator.

The generator used is one of the Siemens' dynamo-electric machines and the motor is the turbine which gives off 6 horse-power; the distance of the turbine and generator from the house is 1,500 yards; the conducting wire is of copper and its section is that of No. 1 Birmingham wire gauge. A return wire of the same material and section is used, so that the current has to pass through 3,000 yards of this wire to complete the circuit . . .

The table lamps were such that they could be switched on and off by lifting off the bowls containing the incandescent lamps, which sat in a pool of mercury. I don't suppose it would pass muster today as the vase supporting the illuminated bowl was made of copper and formed part of the electric circuit!

Lord Armstrong installed two hydraulic lifts in the house and in his conservatory he had fruit trees growing in tubs which were turned by hydraulic power so that all sides of the trees received a share of the sun's rays. These innovations brought British royalty as guests to the house, along with such notable visitors as the Shah of Persia and the Crown Prince of Afghanistan.

Lord Armstrong showed His Highness some of his electric experiments, in the course of which a slight shock was administered to the Prince, which greatly amused him.

47

The Crown Prince of Japan also paid a visit in May 1953 as guest of the Duchess of Northumberland and Lord Percy.

Cragside is well worth a visit though, and even if you find it a vast hotch-potch of periods and style, credit must be given for the attention to detail and magnificent grounds. Lord Armstrong must have found this to be a peaceful retreat from the squalor of the Elswick works in Newcastle.

From the end of Tumbleton Lake rejoin the main road and turn left for Rothbury, which is spread out on the hillside of Coquetdale. Despite its relatively small size, isolated location and surrounding moors and forests, Rothbury has a surprisingly commercial feel to it, the largest buildings being solid Victorian banks. The block which includes the Newcastle Hotel is actually called 'Commercial Buildings'. Down the main street to the left is the bridge over the Coquet with a modern concrete deck superimposed on the old stone piers. The river is as pleasant as its name.

I will sing of the Coquet, the dearest of
themes,
The haunt of the fisher, the first of a'
streams.

(Roxby, 1826)

Rothbury once belonged to King John, but fell into the hands of the Percys like a ripe plum, that is until Robert the Bruce came this way in the fourteenth century.

Hue an' cry – hoond an' horse – ca' to the fray,
For the Scots hae been Rotbarie way i' the murk
An left na a galloway, sheepe, hogge or stirke,
Fired a' the haudins an' harried the Kirk,
Au faur waur them a';
Oh! wae ti'll us wae,
The Meenister's missin', they've lifted him tae.

(Ballad by Joseph Crowhall)

It flourished in Victorian times and continues to do so as a 'getaway' place from Newcastle. (Why does everyone want to escape from Newcastle when it's such a good city in its own right?) Rothbury is in splendid walking country, lying between the volcanic Cheviots and the more hospitable sandstone of the Simonside Hills – perhaps that's the reason.

Leave on the B6341, following the soft green valley of Coquetdale. Along the river you can find a wonderful collection of wild flowers – butterbur with its stubby pink spike and rhubarb-shaped leaves, brooklime, recognised by its small blue flowers and shiny stem, and the more common marsh marigold with large yellow flowers and green leaves.

The main predator of these lonely streams is the otter, although these are now being driven northwards and their place is being taken by the mink. Mink have spread rapidly through Northumbria to the Cheviots following numerous escapes from fur farms.

A great deal of illicit whisky and gin passed through Coquetdale in the nineteenth century. Kegs of Scotch whisky were brought on horseback over the

49

Elsdon Pele

Cheviots in one direction and Dutch gin from Boulmer in the other. But the waters of the Coquet were themselves ideal for distillation, so they made their own illicit whisky with a number of stills, each with an output of about one hundred gallons per week. The smugglers were probably the originators of the various tales that abounded of the hillsides being haunted by mischievous elves with hideous faces, armed with torches and clubs.

Past the villages of Thropton, Warton and Hepple the road veers away from the Coquet and enters harsher country, denoted by the first of many red flags indicating that firing is taking place on the huge military range. Appropriately, the road drops down to the frontier town of Elsdon.

> *If ye've niver been at Elsdon,*
> *   Take ma advice and gan,*
> *For ivery chiel in Elsdon,*
> *   Is ivery inch a man.*
> *Ay, there's decent folk in Elsdon,*
> *   As iver aw did see,*
> *So aw'm away to Elsdon,*
> *   And come alang wi' me.*

> *(Anon.)*

Elsdon was the capital of the Lords of Redesdale before Scotland and England even existed. They were wild people, with no industry or land to work. They relied on raiding, rustling and thieving of every kind to survive. The Merchants of Newcastle ruled that no-one from that area could be granted an apprenticeship, 'the menfolk not being of honest conversation'. Of the many old settlements in the area, only the fortified peles (pronounced 'peels') remain, the finest being in Elsdon. The roadside gibbet was as common a sight then as telephone boxes are today. (Incidentally, why have all the old red boxes in the middle of nowhere been replaced by the slick London-style ones? Presumably because they didn't think it mattered. Put those responsible in the pillories, I say!)

Elsdon Pele, just north of the ancient church of St. Cuthbert, so named after the saint's coffin rested here in 875 AD on its extended journey from Holy Island to Durham, is now privately owned; but despite some alterations it has retained its massive external walls. Built in the fourteenth century, it must have withstood many a battle. In more recent times, as the church vicarage, its main battle was fought against the elements. Two centuries ago the Reverend Dodgson wrote:–

> The vestibule of the Castle is a low stable, and above it is the kitchen in which there are two little beds joining to each other. The curate and his wife lay in one, and Margery, the maid, in the other. I lay in the parlour, between two beds, to keep me from being frozen to death, for, as we keep open house, the winds enter from every quarter, and are apt to creep into bed to one.

The vicar left after three winters but he was lucky compared with his predecessors:–

> Many clergy were reluctant to accept the Elsdon living because they were afraid for their personal safety. In this rude, superstitious people on the Borders, priests go with sword, dagger and such apparel as they can get.

wrote Pilkington, who was Bishop of Durham from 1561 to 1578.

Redesdale's character has been formed by geography and violence. In Roman times, after the building of Hadrian's Wall, it became a buffer zone between the Caledonian clans to the north and the English to the south. Thus the border as it now exists in an artificial one reflecting the ebb and flow of battles and politics. After being over-run, first by the Angles and then the Normans, the geographical border of Scotland became the rivers Tweed and Solway. William the Conqueror ordered the Borders to be an independent Liberty area under the jurisdiction of Lord Redesdale, one of the infamous Umfravilles. It was not until 1328 that England recognised Scotland's independence, but that did not prevent the Barons on both sides of the border carrying on the struggle, two of the great antagonists being Lord Percy and James, Earl of Douglas.

The border tensions created great feuds and rivalries between clans and families, but with too many mouths to feed reiving became a way of life, and the fortress-like peles and castles grew up everywhere, a matter of necessity in the fight against the raiders. Anyone, rich or poor, friend or foe, was fair game.

It is said that on awaking after a night's sleep, a Borderer would first feel his throat to see if it had been slit during the night. Those involved in armed raiding were well aware that, if caught, the punishment was the scaffold and therefore the first essential was to have a good horse. The border horses were small and surefooted, and called bog-trotters. The raiders themselves, 'moss troopers' as they were known, wore a steel hat, leather coat sewn with metal plates, and leather breeches. Their weapons were the lance, sabre, dirk and hand guns, called 'dags'. Attacks were carried out on moonless nights as they knew every inch of the moors. Autumn, being 'good and dry and cattle strong to drive,' was the raiding season – with the gangs usually numbering fifty or so.

Eventually the 'Liberty' was removed, the lairds dismissed, and jurisdiction placed under the Sheriff of Northumberland by Henry VIII. Elizabeth I later dismissed the Lord of Northumberland from the Wardenship and gave the post to Sir John Forster, who brought in off-comers as his officials. He destroyed the troublemakers, took the scheming lairds hostage and exacted heavy ransoms for prisoners. Sir John won the day if not the popularity stakes, but in the end it was the church and education which transformed the population into an honest brotherhood.

> *The last of all the Bards was he,*
> *Who sung of Border chivalry;*
> *For, welladay! their date was*
> * fled,*
> *His tuneful brethren all were dead;*
> *And he, neglected and oppress'd,*
> *Wish'd to be with them, and at*
> * rest.*

(Sir Walter Scott)

The great names of these families live on – the Armstrongs, Eliots, Charltons, Dodds and Milburns, Ridleys, Percys, Nevilles, Reeds and Herons.

Climbing out of the village on the B6341 to Otterburn, the view is spoilt by a coal merchant's yard established, for good reason, on the site of the old mine, but you soon come to pleasant rolling countryside where the road turns at the A696 for Newcastle.

54

Otterburn Tower

Otterburn, once called 'the Emporium of Redesdale', is now dominated by the ubiquitous woollen mill shop, the Percy Arms and the excellent fortress hotel called Otterburn Tower. The otters have long since left the village for quieter habitats away from the main road.

About a mile further north, in a plantation of trees, stands Percy's Cross commemorating the Battle of Otterburn in 1388 where the English were slaughtered by the Scots, led by the Earl of Douglas. Douglas himself was killed in the battle, though his death went unnoticed as he was trampled into the ground, first by the English and then by the Scots as they made their counter attack.

> *My wound is deep; I fain would sleep;*
> *Take thou the vanguard of the three;*
> *And hide me by the braken bush*
> *That grows on yonder lillye lee.*
>
> *Oh! bury me by the braken bush,*
> *Beneath the blooming briar,*
> *Let never a living mortal ken*
> *That ere a kindly Scot lies here.*

More than a thousand of the English were left dead on the field, many with appalling head wounds. The Percy brothers, who led the battle, were both taken prisoner, though later released on paying a ransom.

A mile further on lies Otterburn Camp, it is the headquarters of this vast military training area and artillery range. I remember it well for its ruggedness,

the weather and as a warning of battles yet to be fought rather than a reminder of those past. It was the young Winston Churchill, Home Secretary in the last Liberal (yes, Liberal) Government, who, whilst on holiday, noted that the terrain would make a first class training area for the Army. Some training area – some National Park!

About a mile and a half further along we join the A68, one of the main routes between England and Scotland, renowned for its long straight stretches interspersed with incredible hump-backs. Even at speed it's possible to enjoy the open views of the countryside and you may perhaps glimpse the wild goats of the Cheviots which roam this far. Past Rochester, once a Roman camp, is the Redesdale Barracks with more red flags. The road now runs alongside Redesdale Forest with its pines and spruces.

At Cottonshopeburn there is a sign for the Forest Drive Toll-road to Kielder where our route turns left, but if you have time, then go on a few miles on the switch-back to Carter Bar, where you meet the Scottish border. At the large lay-by there is a viewpoint with a splendid panorama over Scotland. This is the most dramatic of border crossings, 1250 feet high and with a feeling of being 'over the top'.

But back to the Forest Drive. It starts through mature trees as it crosses the River Rede and brings you first to Blakehopeburnhaugh (whew!). As you are warned, this is a forest track, not a metalled road, but the surface is good enough to potter along at thirty miles per hour. At Blakehope Nick the view opens on to Kielder Forest and you realise that this is a special treat with marvellous things to see. If you stop to take photographs you will be watched by the Black and Red Grouse – they will even pose for you.

East Kielder next, and the track passes through forests of varying degrees of maturity. The Forestry Commission have kindly erected boards stating the species of trees and dates of planting. The Sitka spruce planted in 1974 are about twenty feet high. The piles of sawn logs at the roadside serve to remind you that this is a place of work; Norway spruce planted in 1935 are being felled – half a century of growing before harvesting this crop.

The very first tree-planting took place to the south at Falstone in 1926. The bulk of the early planting was spruce, fast growing trees ideally suited to the wet peaty ground. The Sitka spruce is well able to withstand the arctic climate experienced in the Cheviots and accounts for seventy percent of all conifers planted. A further sixteen percent is made up of Norway spruce – the popular Christmas tree which is suited to the lower, more fertile slopes – and the rest, especially where heather previously grew, is mainly Scots pine. If you look hard you will also find a few other species like the Japanese larch with its rosette-shaped cones.

The trees produce high yields of timber – a hundred tons per acre – used for wood pulp and chipboard. Felling is now carried on at the rate of a million trees a year, with 75,000 Christmas trees harvested by lopping the tops off maturing Norway spruce.

With time to explore, there are plenty of walks and trails to follow, but it is as well to remember that June and September are usually the driest months and July and August the warmest. Other outdoor sports include angling (Kielder Water is stocked with brown trout and rainbow trout), sailing, cruising, water-skiing, swimming and horse-riding. Five thousand deer roam the area with the shaggy brown and white wild goats, but be careful of the adders. Perhaps the greatest menace is the special strain of Kielder midge-fly. If you find a repellant to beat the Kielder midge your fortune will be made.

The Forest Drive ends at Kielder Castle, a visitors' centre with research facilities. At Kielder village you can still see the remains of the old railway line from Hexham to Riccarton. There are some who will remember the *Dipper*, a locomotive sent to this line after being involved in the Tay Bridge disaster. After the crash, when the loco was recovered, no Scotsman would drive it again and it was shunted off to this English outpost of the North British Railway.

From the village follow the new road on the south side of the reservoir and from here you can appreciate the full extent of this stupendous man-made lake – all 44 million gallons of it – officially opened by the Queen in 1982. A mile further on you come to the sailing centre at Leaplish, one of several amenities designed very much with tourism and recreation in mind. Just before reaching the dam, which is, incidentally, higher than St. Paul's Cathedral, there is an information centre giving details of the water supply industry in general and Kielder in particular. The dam itself represents modern engineering at its best with its graceful curves and slopes, and despite its enormous size it manages to blend into the scenery like the work of a great artist.

The overall impression of Kielder Water is that man-made landscapes can be good. Some people find such large intrusions unacceptable, but it is hard to see how generations who have not known the area without the dam and reservoir can fail to find it a beautiful and peaceful place for recreation. Its scale allows plenty of room for sailors, anglers, picnickers and other visitors to enjoy themselves without disturbing one another. It is to be hoped that it will never reach the conditions that pertain on Windermere in the Lake District, with its traffic signs, speed limits, 'no go' areas, and so on.

It is ironic that, given the present demand for water, the massive Kielder scheme was probably never necessary. The need for water that was anticipated from new industry, especially on Teesside, never materialised due to the decline of heavy engineering industries in the north, especially since 1979. However, given that it has been built, and despite the water rates, I think that people should get on and enjoy Kielder.

At the junction signposted to Falstone on the left, you can make a choice. If time is short keep on the new road, which will get you to Bellingham more quickly, but if you have time to spare, turn left for Falstone to follow the old road down the valley. This will give you a better feel of what the valley was like before the dam was built. But take note – this is a gated road requiring the willing assistance of a passenger at half a dozen gates, and:–

> *On Kielder-side the wind blaws wide:*
> *There sounds nae hunting horn*
> *That rings sae sweet as the winds that beat*
> *Round the banks where Tyne is born.*
>
> *(Swinburne)*

Falstone is a small village with a suitably sized pub, church and school. The old railway station is now the Forest Office. Apart from the human scale of the village, there are clear views to enjoy from this side of the valley towards Bellingham, but as well as contending with the gates, the road twists and turns as it follows the old railway line. In Lanehead it jinks right and left through the village as the view of the North Tyne valley unfolds. It is particularly attractive if you have the evening sun behind you.

Quite suddenly the road drops down into Bellingham (another –jum). At the T-junction on a sharp bend turn half-left into the town. Compared with some other small towns on this journey, Bellingham is a little disappointing. Arthur

Mee sums it up as a 'plain little' market town. It lacks a focal point or any coherence. There is nothing 'bad' about it but it seems to be short of something positively 'good', perhaps because in its violent past it was burnt and ransacked time and time again.

We re-trace our steps and follow the signs for Wark and Hexham along the B6320 road which crosses the river on a substantial stone bridge with a toll house at its southern end. As the road climbs there is a fine view of Bellingham to the left, set in open rolling pastureland. The road, now tree-lined, winds its way into Wark by the parish church.

In the village there is a pleasant green with a large chestnut tree. On the left are the ever present 'Black Bull' and 'Grey Bull' – even the bank next door is the 'Black Horse'. Wark was once the chief town of Tynedale and the scene of the murder of Alfwald, the last King of Northumbria. He was known as the 'just and pious King', who for nine years followed the Christian way of life and raised the moral standards of his people. No wonder he was assassinated.

From Wark cross the river and head south for Simonburn, which has a stunning simplicity with its open, cottage-lined green, interesting old tithe barn and church of St. Mungo.

At Chollerford follow the complicated road system and cross the narrow bridge, which we shall meet again in the next chapter. The George Hotel has a fine riverside site which is even more magnificent in winter. I know of one couple who actually spent their honeymoon here with the temperature outside at $-8°C$.

You will recognise the approach to Hexham by the steam belching from the chemical works.

King James I and VI (England and Scotland) called Hexham the 'Heart of all England' as he stopped here on his way south to pick up his English crown in

1603. It stands on a raised terrace overlooking the Tyne valley and although it might seem to have some strategic significance, the Romans ignored it. It has flourished on and off through the ages, no doubt for the same reasons it still flourishes today – a protected environment, convenient communications and a good market.

Hexham once belonged to Queen Etheldreada who married one of the Kings of Northumbria, but on refusing to give up her virginity she ended her days as the Abbess of Ely. She gave Hexham to her friend, Wilfrid, who became Archbishop of York and turned the town into an exclusive ecclesiastical kingdom with its own laws and courts.

Not surprisingly life centred on the Priory Church – now known as Hexham Abbey – which also provided protection and deliverance from the Scots and the barbarous reivers.

From the big Wentworth car park where you can stretch your legs, follow the signs to the tourist office located in the Manor Office. It was once the ancient prison, built in 1332 of Roman stone from nearby *Corstopitum*, and it still retains the appearance of its original use; but it is a good place to start a tour of the town.

Walk through the archway, turn right and go along Pudding Chair to the Moot Hall and the Market Place. If you are lucky enough to be here on market day (Tuesday) then you really feel the purpose of the town, not just in its busy market, but because of the endless procession of landrovers and cattle trucks. Market day is very special in Hexham.

On the north side of the market place is the Shambles which is as fascinating as it is simple. If the Romans had built bus stations, surely they would have looked like this. It is interesting to note that the round columns on the south side are stone, whereas those on the north are timber. On non-market days, the market

Kielder Water

place totally loses its bustling vitality and reverts to being a car park.

Walk up Fore Street, through the shops to Battle Hill. At the end of the street on the left is Robbs', a remarkably big department store for a place of this size, perhaps indicative of the money that is spent here. In splendid isolation on an island site is the Midland Bank.

To the right along Battle Hill, on the old main road through the town, there are more shops. This leads into Beaumont Street and then to the park, a delightful setting for the Abbey which dominates the town.

For touring the Abbey it is best to start at Wilfrid's gate which dates from 1140, reminding you that it was founded as an Augustinian Priory. The choir is a text-book piece of the Early English period with its elegant arcade and pointed arches. An abbey of this size and grandeur can have its architecture extolled but not in a few paragraphs. Its beauty has to be experienced. Its medieval paintings and delicate woodwork tracery have to be studied and its font, made from the base of a Roman pillar, wondered at. But for me at least, the magnificent stonework, its setting and its choral music are the virtues which enthral. And if you have ever heard the Northumbrian pipes (like bagpipes, but the bag is squeezed and not blown) played in such an atmosphere – well, there's something you'll never forget.

Hexham suffered bitterly at the hands of the Scots and in 1296 was burnt to the ground, including the Abbey, whose priceless treasures were purloined. Even the school full of children was sealed up and rased to the ground. Again and again the town and Abbey were ravaged; again and again they were rebuilt. In 1761, during the Civil War, the 'Hexham Riot' took place, having had its origins in Durham. A crowd of five thousand had assembled in the market place and were faced by 240 troops of the North York Militia. The Riot Act was read out, and when the

Hexham Abbey

crowd refused to disperse the soldiers opened fire, killing fifty-one and wounding three hundred more. One man, Patterson, who was not even in the market square that day, was arrested, tried and hanged. When on the scaffold, the rope broke and he called out, 'Innocent blood is ill to shed!'

> *Vengeance, deep-brooding o'er the slain,*
> *Had lock'd the source of softer woe;*
> *And burning pride and high disdain*
> *Forbade the rising tear to flow.*
>
> *(Sir Walter Scott)*

The vengeance is gone now, but pride remains, together with the rising tear. The Borders flourish in their beauty and ruggedness.

CHAPTER THREE

Hadrian's Wall

EMPEROR HADRIAN'S WALL

EMPEROR HADRIAN'S WALL

CORBRIDGE – CHESTERS – HOUSESTEADS – VINDOLANDA
(Distance 20 miles)
(See Ordnance Survey special map – Hadrian's Wall)

Humpty Dumpty sat on a wall;
Humpty Dumpty had a Great Fall!

The Roman invasion of Britain by Julius Caesar in the first century AD was aimed at subduing the barbarians of this wild country. But it was left to Emperor Hadrian in the next century to create the wall we can now see stretching across Northumbria from Newcastle to Carlisle – equal in significance to the Great Wall of China or, in more recent times, the frontier between East and West Germany. Ninety miles long, fifteen feet high, and ten feet thick with six-foot parapets, it was manned by 50,000 Legionaries, families and camp followers for nearly three centuries before the Romans finally withdrew.

The barren land and scenery is little changed since the cohorts left, and the remains of the greatest system of fortifications in Europe have become a tourist attraction of immense size, though twenty years ago they were hardly known except to archaeologists.

Romanisation and fraternisation left their mark on the population, always small in number, though the buildings must have outnumbered the Romans many times over.

As an effective military obstacle, the wall had to be heavily manned or it would soon have been overrun. Even so, its sheer length meant that a rapid means of transferring soldiers and supplies along the wall was vital. It was for this reason that a military way was built alongside the fortress-like wall – a road we shall follow in this chapter on our trek along the wall, on the B6318, re-aligned and re-named the Military Road.

Travelling east to west and omitting the first section at Wallsend and the great City of Newcastle, we begin at the village of Corbridge on the River Tyne. It is with good reason that we start our journey here, for this was the great road junction with the Roman road from London, Watling Street/Dere Street, where it crossed the Tyne. Its position ensured that it became one of the largest Roman stations in the north and the site of a huge central stores and headquarters, *Corstopitum*.

The position of Corbridge, its proximity to Newcastle and ease of access, has ensured its prosperity, though now more as a commuter village and tourist attraction. It was from here that the Lancastrians were launched into the battle of Hexham with such disastrous results, and where, in the tenth century, the Danes won an important victory. In the twelfth century, Corbridge was captured by the Scots, who tried to incorporate it into Scotland, then, having failed to achieve their object, burnt it to the ground instead, twice – once by Robert the Bruce in 1312.

> *Our bugles sang truce – for the night-cloud*
>   *had lowered,*
> *And the sentinel stars set their watch in the sky;*
> *And thousands had sunk on the ground*
>   *overpowered,*
> *The weary to sleep, and the wounded to die.*
>
> *(Thomas Campbell)*

King John came here three times around 1200, perhaps to bolster the flagging spirits of the Northumbrians but more likely, and on good evidence, to search for the treasure – a substantial hoard – which he had been told was buried here.

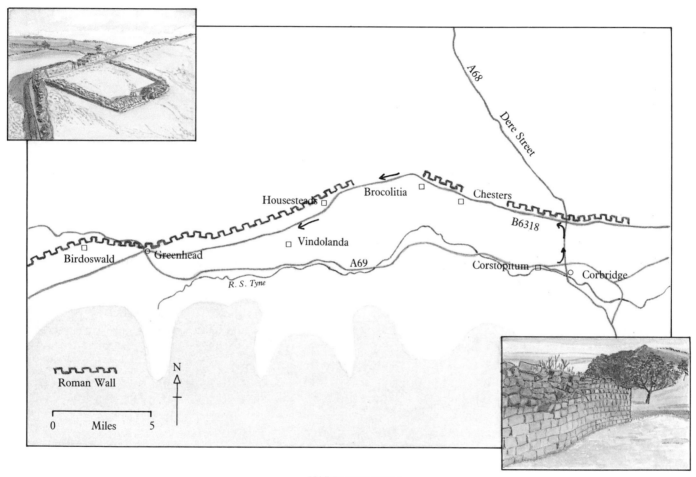

A68

Dere Street

Housesteads Brocolitia Chesters

B6318

Vindolanda

Birdoswald Greenhead A69 Corstopitum Corbridge

R. S. Tyne

Roman Wall

N

0 Miles 5

HADRIAN'S WALL

However, except for some bronze, iron and lead pieces, he went away empty-handed. His excavations may have been ineffective but his information was certainly accurate, for this century has revealed two caches of gold coins, and not long ago a young girl dug up a silver salver on the banks of the Tyne near the bridge. These are now in the British Museum in London, but word has it that the bulk of the treasure thought to be there is hidden along the river bank and not far from the bridge. Not, perhaps, the seven-arched one you see today, which was only built in 1673, but further upstream where the line of the river has changed. The remains of the Roman bridge, made of wooden trusses resting on ten piers of masonry, can still be seen when the water is low enough.

The role of Corbridge in the past can hardly be exaggerated, first as a centre of road communications, then as a headquarters for the Legion's mobile cavalry, and finally as the primary store base of northern Britain. Now it's all antique shops, Watling Street Tea Rooms and cars. Leave by the Wheatsheaf Inn with its brightly painted cart on display, and away to the nerve centre of the Roman Headquarters at *Corstopitum*, a short distance to the north, just off the A68.

The old Nissen hut I once knew has been replaced by a low, modern museum, full of artefacts dug up over the years. The camp is beautifully set in a shallow bowl, surrounded by hills which are partly covered with conifers and has lovely views over the river. Such is the atmosphere here that it is possible to peer into the mists of space and time and pick out the ghosts of those mail-clad, helmeted soldiers from the past. You can easily imagine yourself recently arrived from London or York to visit your troops or perhaps to join your husband, together with children, in his new posting. What's the weather like compared with Rome? And the schools and shops? Like Army families everywhere, they would have made the best of it.

Ah! gentle, fleeting, wav'ring sprite,
Friend and associate of this clay!
To what unknown region borne,
Wilt thou now wing thy distant flight?
No more with wonted humour gay,
But pallid, cheerless, and forlorn.

(Emperor Hadrian)

The Stanegate road that ran from the base at *Corstopitum* to Carlisle is not the same as the military road that runs alongside the wall. We can see Stanegate at the fort, which was originally built by Julius Agricola and housed one of the cavalry regiments. Later the craftsmen came – masons, toolmakers, leather-workers, as well as merchants and farmers, all catering for the needs of the garrison and trading with the natives north and south of the border.

The buildings you see now were constructed later than the wall, which is half a mile to the north, and include workshops, offices, meeting rooms, storehouses and granaries. Troops with families were provided with married-quarters, schools, bath-houses and latrines. A chapel was built over the strongroom, which was supported on huge pillars and incorporated clerestory windows to give more light.

Walk through the substantial remains, through the one-acre storehouse and across the granaries with loading bays and access roads. The extraordinary wave effect of the ground levels creates rippled walls and a sensation of being at sea, but closer examination reveals a network of municipal drains, aqueducts and a fountain. The stones around the fountain are worn where the soldiers sharpened their knives, swords and axes.

Wall and Fort, Vindolanda

Inside the small museum there are large quantities of cooking utensils, pottery, combs, cow bells, surgeons' knives, gardening tools, coloured glass fragments of deep blue, brown, yellow and green, and even inkpots of the unspillable type we used to have at school.

The four Legions chosen to carry out the invasion and establish the defences were Roman born and bred, but they brought with them European auxiliaries, from Spain, France and Germany. The strength of the Legions lay in their professionalism, discipline and devotion to the Emperor.

The first invasion by Julius Caesar in 55 BC had cost the Romans dearly when faced with the chariots of the 'barbarians'. Claudius, too, had had his difficulties between 43–60 AD, having been seen off by the British warrior queen, Boadicea, who massacred 70,000 Roman soldiers.

While about the shore of Mona those Neronian legionaries
Burnt and broke the grove and altar of the Druid and Druidesses,
Far in the East Boadicea, standing loftily charioted,
Mad and maddening all that heard her in her fierce volubility,
Yell'd and shriek'd between her daughters o'er a wild
    confederacy . . .

There the horde of Roman robbers mock at a barbarous adversary,
There the hive of Roman liars worship an emperor-idiot.
Such is Rome, and this her deity . . .

There they drank in cups of emerald, there at tables of ebony lay,
Rolling on their purple couches in their tender effeminacy,

There they dwelt and there they rioted; there – there – they
* dwell no more.*
Burst the gates, and burn the palaces, break the works of the
* statury,*
Take the hoary Roman head and shatter it, hold it abominable . . .

Out of evil evil flourishes, out of tyranny tyranny buds.
Ran the land with Roman slaughter, multitudinous agonies.
Perish'd many a maid and matron, many a valorous legionary,
Fell the colony, city, and citadel, London, Verulam, Camulodúne.

(Lord Tennyson)

Hadrian was taking no chances when he came. He brought his finest troops from Germany, but he also applied more subtle methods. As well as the mailed fist he brought sophistication, technology and trade to further his plans for the Romanisation of Britain. He brought entertainment, the bathing pool, and religion to replace the form of Druidism prevalent in England.

At first the settlements around the fort took the rather primitive form of a collection of wattle and clay huts outside the camp gates to provide opportunities for the soldiers to fraternise. These huts, wigwam-like in appearance, were popular and provided the equivalent of wine bars, brothels, cockpits and casinos, as well as shops to trade in food, spices and trinkets.

Return to the A68 and journey northwards through the rich, green, rolling countryside lined with beech and oak. At the Errington Arms turn left on to the B6318.

Bathhouse, Chesters

The Military Road, or the 'Military' as it is known locally, was built on its present alignment by Army engineers in 1752–3 to improve the mobility of army units from east to west following Bonnie Prince Charlie's rapid invasion down the western flank. Unfortunately they built it of stone taken from Hadrian's Wall and in doing so destroyed much of the wall.

With the Cheviots in the distance to the right (snow-capped for some months each year), we travel parallel to the 'ditch' and 'vallum' – like huge anti-tank ditches – partially water-filled and lined with gorse. The road, which for much of the time is on top of the wall, is absolutely straight. At Chollerford it has been re-aligned to allow for a crossroads and the construction of a bridge by the well-known George Inn.

If, like me, you feel impatient for a proper sight of the wall, don't let this spoil your enjoyment of the open landscape, far hills, and the wonder of the huge earthworks of the vallum and ditch.

Ah! Here we are at Chesters fort. Quiet, except for the rushing river glinting all silver in the sun, surrounded by ancient oaks. If Chesters (*Cilurnum*) was the fort that soldiers regarded as a rest cure it is not surprising. It covered nearly six acres of the finest scenery along the North Tyne valley, all on a south-facing slope. Naturally, it was commandeered by the elite cavalry as their headquarters, and the commandant's home befits his exalted position. On the other side of the river you can make out the stone abutments of the old timber bridge the Romans built.

But the bath-house by the river is the real gem at Chesters. It is complete – the foundtions, that is – showing the changing room, latrines, hot rooms, cold rooms, warm rooms, cold baths, hot baths and so on. Almost all Romans took a daily bath, it being a social event, like coffee, tea and dinner parties! The central heating system was by means of hot air from furnaces at one end which was then

Emperor Hadrian's Wall

led through stone ducts to warm the rooms above. For dry heat they used carbon or charcoal, and for wet heat, wood and peat.

Try to picture the scene as you walk through the huge porch into a large communal changing room nearly fifty feet by thirty feet, with lavatory on the left (discharging into the river downstream) and shrines for worshipping the gods on the right. Having undressed, they passed through a series of bath rooms where they could take their pick – hot bath, cold bath, warm–moist, hot–dry. It was possible to dash or wander from one to another and on the way be massaged with oils, scraped with knives, sponged and pummelled.

Mixed bathing was forbidden, but judging by the number of women's hairgrips and pieces of jewelry found by archaeologists in the drains, it happened by common consent. Whether they were wives or camp followers is not known, but possibly they were bussed in from York as a sort of peripatetic bathing troupe.

By the River

> There by none of beauty's daughters
>   With a magic like thee;
> And like music on the waters
>   Is thy sweet voice to me:
> When, as if its sound were causing
> The charméd ocean's pausing,
> The waves lie still and gleaming,
> And the lulled winds seem dreaming.

(Lord Byron)

Back on the 'military', deserted for most of the year, you can see the serrated hills ahead. There is a sharp turn in the road to the left, called Limestone Corner, where the vallum ditch is deeply cut into the rocks. Shortly after is the ancient monument sign to the Temple of Mithras at Carrawburgh (*Brocolitia*). The temple was first explored in 1876 along with Coventina's Well, which was thought to have been filled with rubbish.

They discovered a well. It is a good spring, and the receptacle for the water is about seven foot square within, and built on all sides, with hewn stone; the depth could not be known when I saw it, because it was almost filled up with rubbish. There had also been a wall about it, or an house built over it, and some of the great stones belonging to it were yet lying there. The people called it a cold bath, and rightly judged it to be Roman.

Some rubbish! It contained 13,490 Roman coins, altar incense burners and even a bronze Scottie dog trinket. The coins had been thrown into the well – as is still done in Rome and all over the world – to appease the gods or consciences. They were from the reign of Emperor Antonius Pius who succeeded Hadrian.

The path leads to the Mithraic temple and disappointment. Much of it has been removed to Newcastle and replaced with mock-ups, which can never be quite the same.

We hurry on to Housesteads now, along the 'military', which veers away from the wall. Along this straight road there are no signs of life except for lone crows, a few brave sheep and a glistening tarn to the left. BUT YOU CAN SEE THE WALL, clinging to the ridges of the hills a short distance away. Definitely the Great Wall of China is your first thought. But steady on, just past the 'Beggar Bog' turn right into Housesteads car park.

Latrine, Housesteads Fort

Whether you come to Housesteads in June or January you will be struck by the solitude, but even more so by the mysterious atmosphere that pervades these stony hills and plains. It is a haunting sensation that makes it easy to visualise the ghosts of a busy Roman garrison, noisy with the comings and goings of the soldiers. Outside there was a thriving, bustling shopping and agricultural market town. When the garrison was a thousand strong there must have been two thousand outside the walls of the fort. The Roman name of VERCOVICIUM means 'hilly place', and so it is, making the views from the ramparts all the more exciting.

The fort covers an area of five acres and the town twice that amount. It was occupied for a period of about three hundred years from 120 AD, when Emperor Hadrian decided he must have a forward defensive position here. Though overrun many times, it was not destroyed until the final onslaught in 400 AD by the Caledonians from the north, after which it became a Christian settlement established by St. Cuthbert.

As with other military garrisons, the wives and children of the soldiers lived there and some soldiers even retired there after completing their twenty-five years' service in the Legion – a situation not much different from the British Army today, except that we live to be twice their age.

Now it's time for action. Car in the car park, walking boots firmly tied, anoraks and sweaters on, rain gear at the ready (but forget umbrellas if you wish to remain earthbound), and off we go on our inspection of the fort and on patrol to reconnoitre the wall.

Approaching the fort, the plaintive shouts of the rooks echoing from a coppice on the right can make you believe the Romans are still in occupation. Imagine you are the Emperor himself, or a Centurion, or perhaps a Centurion's wife, just

arrived from Rome, London or Belgium. You've come to see for yourself.

Looking north towards the fort are the city settlements scattered over the hillside, with shops, churches, wine bars, hotels and workshops. The remains are there; you only have to use your imagination a little.

You pass a small spring first where there is fresh water and a pool. Once there was a temple here and in 1961 treasure was found – coins and a coin-making mould. Was it gold? Counterfeit, the experts say. Cheating the gods? What next? Well, there have always been robbers here. Even the historian Camden wrote in 1600:–

> I could not with safety take the full survey of it for the rank robbers thereabouts.

Go first to the museum to see the artefacts and Roman altars, but don't waste time; there is much to do. Nowhere else in Britain will you find such an extensive and well preserved Roman fort, which is why it's a Mecca to historians, archaeologists and tourists from America and Europe. Superb stretches of the wall on either side, a glorious setting and an atmosphere made for the imagination.

Enter the compound, past the well by the south gate of the fort, turn right and head for the latrines. This is a large stone building with no screens or divisions, channels carved out of the rock on either side leading to deeper sewers, a row of army-issue thunder-boxes on either side over the channels. It was all flushed away with water from the storage tanks outside. Down the hillside it went and then it was led into irrigation ditches by the enterprising market gardeners who sold the crops back to the army!

Walk north-west along the VIA PRINCIPALIS and enter the Commandant's nineteen-roomed mansion, formed villa-like with a central courtyard. It had all the usual facilities – bath, central heating, reception rooms, bedrooms, kitchen and stabling. Now continue along the *Via Principalis* with the barrack rooms to your right and the headquarters on the left. Perhaps imagine the adjutant standing outside HQ with the standard bearers, with the camp hospital, its wards, operating rooms and treatment rooms ranged behind.

Further along the main street you will find the granaries and the bath-house, the latter not as elaborate as the one in Chesters.

It is an atmosphere in which the ghosts of soldiers may be seen going about their business. Sword drill with the clash of metal blades, wrestling, archery, and the inevitable spit and polish, breastplates gleaming in the sun. The place is crowded. Sheep, horses and carts laden with wheat and straw, bullock carts, children getting under foot and NCO's shouting commands everywhere. The poor and the sick lie patiently at the gates hoping for a copper or two, hands out, perishing cold. The blacksmiths are hard at it, beating swords into ploughshares and vice versa. There is an all pervading smell of oil, garlic, perfume, spices, dung and woodsmoke.

Oh yes, over there is the butcher's shop. Beef, mutton, wild boar, venison, pigeon and grouse. Plenty to choose from and a daily supply of fresh fish from the river. Cooking was mainly done in pots and bronze pans over a charcoal or wood fire. Juding by the size of the kitchens, dinner parties were not uncommon.

Back to the gods. Jupiter must have been supreme, since nine shrines and dedications to him have been found, with Mithras ranking second and Herion, the Sun God, third. It's not surprising the latter got least support, for in those days – and in these – you worship the god who produces the best results. 'By their fruits ye shall know them.'

Hadrian's Wall

Outside the north-eastern corner of the fort, by Knag Burn, there are the remains of an amphitheatre dished out of the rock, the excavated stone used on the wall, but your eyes will be taken by the wall running eastwards.

By the way, you will see the ruts made by the carts, worn into the stone as you come in at the main entrance, but do measure them. Four feet eight-and-a-half inches between wheels. Strike a chord? It's the gauge used as the standard on our railways, a measurement which George Stephenson took from the horse-drawn coal wagons – another Roman legacy.

We have to begin our patrol of the wall. After all, it's the WALL that this journey is about and we've hardly seen it yet. And it's not just a wall, nothing as simple as that. When Hadrian first designed it, it was to be twenty-one feet high to the top of the crenellated parapet and ten feet thick. In front there was to be a fighting ditch, thirteen feet deep and thirty feet wide with the excavated material being spread to give a forward slope in front of the ditch. Behind the wall – sometimes as much as four hundred yards behind – there was a vallum, a twenty-foot wide, eight foot deep ditch, the function of which is unknown. It would have made an excellent tank trap! At every mile along the ninety-mile wall was a fortlet called a milecastle.

Today the method of construction would be by continuous operation, beginning at Carlisle and moving steadily eastwards to Wallsend (with the wind behind). The wall, ditch and vallum would come out in perfect lines behind the construction train. But no military engineer would build like that, then or now. The ninety-mile line would have been divided into three major sectors, East, West and Central, each under a commander. Each sector would be sub-divided into three further sub-sections, making nine in all. Each section commander would appoint separate teams for quarrying, transporting and laying stone. There would have been one section of surveyors responsible for measuring and marking out the entire route. A quick calculation shows that there was a total of two million tons of stone used and ten million cubic yards of digging.

Forget the wind and the weather, but watch for the arrows of the marauders from the north as you set forth, hand on sword and heart pounding beneath your breastplate.

> *O, Wild West Wind, thou breath of Autumn's being,*
> *Thou, from whose unseen presence the leaves dead*
> *Are driven, like ghosts from an enchanter fleeing . . .*
>
> *Wild Spirit, which art moving every where;*
> *Destroyer and preserver; hear, O, hear.*
>
> *(Shelley)*

It's an energetic, but not a long walk, and fantastic is not an exaggerated description. From the north-west corner of the fort, clamber on to the six-foot wide wall and follow it westwards through the pine trees. It's as well to have a head for heights, for if you look down you will see you are on a hundred-foot sheer crag. Away to the right Wark Forest can be seen and the ill-fated and largely abandoned Spadeadam 'blue-streak' rocket station.

Out of the trees, the birds twitter all the way. Meadow pipits, I think, but they never stay still long enough for you to study them. You hear many languages on this international causeway – French, Japanese, American and Geordie.

The wall drops sharply to a gateway – another international crossroads, the

Pennine Way, where a different breed of travellers nowadays carry Wainwright books instead of an Ordnance Survey map.

Down a chimney (and if you find a black biro, it's mine please), up a rock face and on the wall again, marching through dappled clouds, wind and sun. You will know by the sign when you reach Hotbank, where we take the Military Way back across the fields, but you will want to go on, drawn by the wall falling and climbing over Crag Lough just ahead. Turn here all the same, and follow the Roman way back, for it's along this track that you obtain the most extensive and satisfying view of the wall stretching for miles and miles. The road is grass-covered and hoof-marked. Roman horses, no doubt. Glorious!

And so back to Housesteads and the car park.

Continue your journey along the 'military', which turns into a switchback with two severe dips, but before you reach the hamlet of 'Twice Brewed', turn left by the Once Brewed Visitor Centre to VINDOLANDA, a fort which housed the 4th Cohort of Gauls in the third century. Whereas Housesteads was all peace, apart from the tribes, *Vindolanda* is a hive of activity, with excavations proceeding apace under the careful eyes of the Birley family. So far as Roman history and Hadrian's Wall are concerned, Professor Eric Birley of Durham University was the father of it all. Robin, his son, directs operations at *Vindolanda*, with teams of students and other enthusiasts who act as diggers. Professor Birley once said to me that the organisation was more important than the individual, but he and his sons confute that argument – their contribution is unique.

Why isn't *Vindolanda* on the line of the wall instead of fifteen hundred yards to the south? The answer to that is that like *Corstopitum*, it was a supply base on the lateral route of the Stanegate, built before the wall as part of the northern defences of the country.

Chesterholm Museum

Situated on a plateau and covering three-and-a-half acres, the fort included the usual barracks, stables, hospitals, granaries, headquarters, bath-house, married-quarters and a hotel for visitors. The buildings, with substantial remains, are highlighted by a full-scale replica of the wall, complete with tower, and catapult.

Outside the fort the civilian town covered some ten acres. There was an extensive tannery and saddlery, for large quantities of leather off-cuts have been found, well preserved by the wet, acid soil. The same conditions have also preserved numerous wooden writing tablets, altars and artefacts.

The museum and cafe are across a tumbling stream, in gardens filled with rhododendrons, conifers and daffodils set against a backdrop of wooded crags and beech trees. A stone arch bridge and timber footbridge complete this idyllic scene.

In the Chesterholm Museum you will see love motifs in the form of pocket Venuses, a Medusa ring, combs, hairpins and a mock-up chariot, but the centrepiece is a full size reproduction of Roman life, complete with sound effects and lighting. A house kitchen with mother cooking, baby in basket crib, large water pots (*amphori*), herbs hanging to dry beside wild ducks and pheasants, and a besom in the corner. Marcus and Materna live here with children Victor and Ursa, and of course the family dog. Breakfast of porridge and fruit is eaten to the accompaniment of bugles from the fort. Over the fire the duck is roasting, to be eaten with herb sauce and then cubes of bread and dates fried in oil. There is a carpet of bracken on the floor, iron household tools, oil lamps and an aroma of spices and fig sauce.

Also in the museum are the fragments of wooden writing tablets. 'I came to Vindolanda and undertook the audit,' one of them translates. No doubt from the

91

Inland Revenue. An intelligence report circa 95 AD refers to 'Brittunculi', or 'wretched Britons'.

And – on a note to raise some eyebrows – there are graffiti carvings euphemistically described as 'phallic symbols'.

It is the remains of the civilian town that make *Vindolanda* so interesting, with the possibility of the whole site being excavated and restored, showing the houses, blacksmith's, plumber's, ironfounder's, shops, joiner's and builder's yards.

Language must have been a problem with troops arriving from Rome, Germany, France and Belgium, as well as the local auxiliaries from England and Scotland, but generally they spoke Latin, as British soldiers of this century have 'spoken' German, Arabic or Punjabi. They managed. So well, in fact, that judging by the inscriptions and writing tablets they must have had some formal teaching in Latin. Perhaps on the dark evenings, when the teachers had finished school for the children, they undertook extra-mural language classes.

The lower classes drank a vinegary type of beer; the upper classes drank wine. Honey was plentiful. Divorce was popular. Women had equal rights, at least until Christianity came to the region. Equal rights in death too, for few lived to be more than forty.

If you don't like the desolation to the north of the wall, here it's different – soft, lush pastures sloping gently towards the river, and not far away are the villages of Bardon Mill and Beltingham. When I first came here thirty years ago by steam train along the Tyne Valley, I thought it was the prettiest place I'd ever seen. It doesn't surprise me to read that Beltingham is named as the most beautiful hamlet in the whole of Northumbria. In the churchyard you can see two Roman altars from *Vindolanda* and the oldest yew tree in Britain, nearly a thousand years old, though my friend the vicar has his doubts! It was here in 1973 that tribute was belatedly paid to the martyr Nicholas Ridley, born close to Hadrian's Wall and baptised here in 1500 AD. He was burnt at the stake in Oxford, along with Cranmer and Latimer, for his Protestant faith on the orders of Bloody Mary Tudor, daughter of Henry VIII. Nancy Ridley says that on that day in 1973 Beltingham was 'thrang' (busy), with even a 'Polis' to control the traffic.

This is a perfect place to end the day, even to spend a whole day, but you can always come back for more. We end our journey here.

If you want to explore more of the wall, then go on to Birdoswald and see the fort designed specifically for the cavalry and occupied by the infantry of Hadrian's 1st Cohort of Dacians. Some claim it to be King Arthur's Camelot, too. Who knows what treasure might be buried there?

We've finished with the Romans, but just consider for a moment those soldiers. Most died where they fell, usually with no headstone. Stripped bare by the natives, mourned by their comrades. No memorial is left.

The Roman Army went home leaving the wall behind. Yet the wall is as important today as it ever was, though for different reasons. If it failed in war, its success in peace, for scholars and tourists, is profound. The Roman soldier left his mark on the Kingdom of Northumbria and that mark, the Wall, will never be erased.

'Tis time this heart should be unmoved,
  Since others it hath ceased to move:
Yet, though I cannot be beloved,
  Still let me love!

93

My days are in the yellow leaf;
  The flowers and fruits of love are gone;
The worm, the canker, and the grief
  Are mine alone!

If thou regret'st thy youth, why live?
  The land of honourable death
Is here:– up to the field, and give
  Away thy breath!

Seek out – less often sought than found –
  A soldier's grave, for thee the best;
Then look around, and choose thy ground,
  And take thy rest.

(Lord Byron)

CHAPTER FOUR

Killhope Wheel, Weardale

DURHAM

DURHAM'S ANCIENT SPLENDOUR

WEARDALE – STANHOPE – BISHOP AUCKLAND – DURHAM CITY
(Distance 45 miles)

J.B. Dykes
Canon of Durham Cathedral
Vicar of St. Oswald's, Durham

From east to west, from shore to shore,

Let eve-ry heart a-wake and sing.

Grey towers of Durham
Yet well I love thy mixed and massive piles
Half church of God, half castle 'gainst the Scot,
And long to roam these venerable aisles
With records stored of deeds long since forgot.

(Sir Walter Scott)

A vast hunting preserve for Prince Bishops, a mining industry and a fortress-like capital city and cathedral are the historical springs of development of Durham, a county with an area of a thousand square miles and a million people.

But the mines have gone and the Bishops have been subdued (almost). Today we have vast heather-clad moors, a tourist industry which has not yet overwhelmed the inhabitants, and a cathedral city as magnificent as ever. This is a county of contrasts, splendour and squalor maybe. Boring – never!

The common thread running through it all, past and present, is the river, the Wear, which rises in the western hills and flows eastwards, gouging its way first through the Pennine moors, on through pastureland, then giving its moat-like protection to the cathedral before going on to Washington, Sunderland and finally the North Sea.

Take that journey along the river, for it encapsulates every aspect of Durham life and history. Never doubt, though, the fierce pride and affection of the people for their cathedral city, whatever their religious beliefs. They can say without fear of contradiction, 'A'll defy ye to beat that!'

So let us begin at the head of Weardale, on the A689 between Alston and St. John's Chapel, where the western border of Durham is clearly marked. Usually in cloud, often in snow, the scene on the top of the Pennines is one of open, desolate country, derelict cottages and scattered, tumbledown farms. Where the homesteads are still inhabited, smoke issues from their chimneys even at the height of summer. Brave clumps of trees survive – oaks, beeches, sycamores and the ubiquitous, tenacious rowans, red with berries.

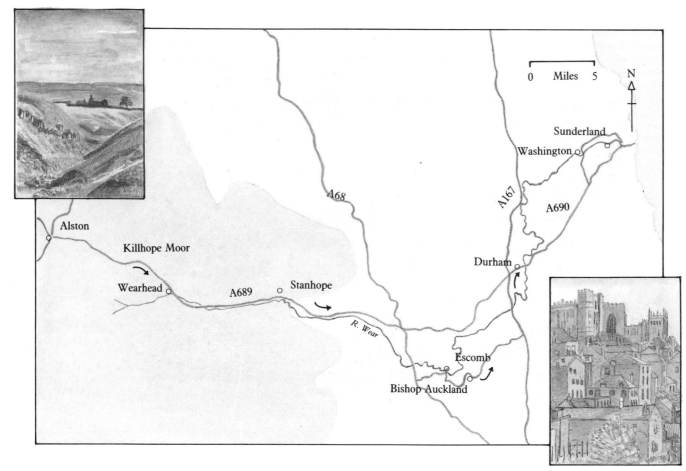

Alston

Killhope Moor

Wearhead   A689   Stanhope

A68

R. Wear

Escomb

Bishop Auckland

Sunderland

Washington

A167   A690

Durham

0   Miles   5

N

DURHAM AND WEARDALE

Relics of abandoned lead mines are scattered across this harsh landscape, grotesque monuments to man's industry, a pit heap here, a smelting chimney there. Bleak rolling moors, distant Pennine peaks. The deserted road is lined with six-foot tall snow marker posts; it may be summer now, but you have been warned!

Summer and Winter

It was a bright and cheerful afternoon,
Towards the end of the sunny month of June,
When the north wind congregates in crowds
The floating mountains of the silver clouds
From the horizon – and the stainless sky
Opens beyond them like eternity.
All things rejoiced beneath the sun; the weeds,
The river, and the corn-fields, and the reeds;
The willow leaves that glanced in the light breeze
And the firm foliage of the larger trees.

It was a winter such as when birds die
In the deep forests; and the fishes lie
Stiffened in the translucent ice, which makes
Even the mud and slime of the warm lakes
A wrinkled clod as hard as brick; and when,
Among their children, comfortable men
Gather about great fires, and yet feel cold:
Alas then for the homeless beggar old!

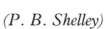

(P. B. Shelley)

99

Upper Weardale with ruined farmhouse

Miners in the nineteenth century used to go to work on skis, so if you enjoy skiing you'd like it here in winter, but otherwise enjoy the exhilaration and mystery of the lonely road as you drive eastwards to the first port of call, the Killhope lead mine, where they've built a museum across the stream, with a huge forty-foot iron wheel which powered a lead crushing mill in 1860. In the reconstructed living quarters – for the men and boys lived on site – imagine yourself as one of the miners who slept six to a bed (plus mice) whilst the speculators made a fat living from the lead which had a high silver content and was used for coinage.

The ore's awaitin' in the tubs, the snow's upon the fell,
Canny folks are sleepin' yet but lead is reet to sell.
Come my little washer lad, come let's away,
We're bound down to slavery for fourpence a day.

It's early in the morning, we rise at five o'clock,
And the little slaves come to the door to knock, knock, knock.
Come my little washer lad, come let's away,
It's very hard to work for fourpence a day.

It must have been a hard life, and a short one by all accounts.

What did they eat, these miners, besides the occasional sheep? Pan Haggerty, I expect. A delicious meal made in the frying pan with dripping, layers of thinly sliced potatoes, onions and cheese, topped with a layer of potatoes browned under the grill.

The journey eastwards on the A689 past Cowshill, with its waterfall, provides a panoramic view down the valley and brings you to Wearhead, where the River Wear officially begins. At Ireshopeburn stop for a moment. Next to the chapel, in which Wesley himself preached, a museum has been created by elderly residents who play the parts of 'exhibits', curators and attendants – a living museum of how things were a hundred years ago, white-bonnetted women ironing with flat irons in a Victorian kitchen. Go in and join them for a cup of tea.

Then on through Weardale, once the hunting preserve of the Bishops of Durham, to St. John's Chapel – a gloomy village – then Daddry Shield and Westgate. Ignore the cement works with its snake-like conveyor belt leading from the limestone crusher at the top of the hill to the furnace near the road. Ignore, too, the veneer of white dust on the trees, houses and people, and get through this 'satanic mill' to the open fields of Eastgate where the river, rabbits and sheep all frolic and tiny weasels dart into the road.

At Stanhope market place you can see the 250-million-year-old fossilised tree stump in the grounds of the beautiful old church opposite the Pack Horse Inn. The market was established by Bishop Langley in 1421.

When you reach Wolsingham, a village once noted for its steelworks, now more for its unemployment, there's an enormous sign with an arrow pointing right to CROOK. Don't follow it, go straight on. On the bench beneath the sign an old man in a cap rests with his border terrier. 'E'll kill any living thing, will that 'un!' Others prefer whippets, which they use for hunting like the Bishops before them.

There is another sign on a bank above the road to Lanchester which reads:–

> Near this spot Venerable John Duckett was arrested.
> He was afterwards tried at Sunderland and taken to
> Tyburn where he was executed for being a priest
> Sep. 7th 1644.

Durham

But let's go on.

At the junction with the A68 turn right and travel past the Duke of York's Inn at Fir Tree. This is Dere Street, absolutely straight as all Roman roads, with extensive views over low-spread purple hills and dark green pine forests. Pass over the River Wear, wider and deeper as it flows through the grounds of Witton Castle, once a ruin, now a leisure centre.

Turn left off the A68 on to a minor road leading to Woodside, a pit village where they take the sun at the front door and keep their racing pigeons at the back. Turn left again to Escomb. A diversion? At first sight another semi-derelict pit village. Twenty years ago it was condemned to death by the planners and county councillors – Category 'D', commonly known as 'death'. A village where, because the pit had closed, the inhabitants were 'encouraged' to move out, which they did. Now they've come back and the village is beginning to thrive. Just one of the mysteries of Escomb.

Why have we come here? No picture postcard village this. But look, a church! Not just any church – a tall Saxon church, built thirteen hundred years ago, it still survives and is still in use. Why was it built and for whom? None can say. What the archaeologists do know is that without doubt it was built by Celtic and Anglo-Saxon builders between 670–690 AD, and that many of the stones in its walls have Roman inscriptions on them. These almost certainly came from the Roman camp, *Vinovia*, two miles away. They commemorate the legion Leg VI which first came over with Hadrian.

The church has two sundials, one of which is the oldest surviving in England. Inside this whitewashed mystery, history and prayer penetrate your bones. Outside, more mystery in the graveyard. Two headstones carved with skull and crossbones. Victims of the plague? Pirates? Spies?

Wolsingham

Return to the A6073 and follow the signs to Bishop Auckland. Make straight for the Palace of the Bishops of Durham, a lovely palace in which to live or to visit. The gateway (or is it a Gothic folly?) points to its use as a baronial hall rather than a fortress.

However, we have come to see the deer in Bishop Auckland park and to watch the Wear thread its way through eight hundred acres of lush green fields – the finest landscaped park in the north. Visit the Deer House, an architectural masterpiece constructed in stone by Bishop Trevor in 1760. It has a courtyard, a cloister and a tower. No need to work it out:–

> Inner courtyard for feeding,
> External cloisters for shelter,
> Tower for hunting parties to rest.

No need either to hunt the deer – they are tame!

> There are two kings in England, namely the King of England wearing a crown in sign of his regality, and the Bishop of Durham wearing a mitre in place of a crown in sign of his regality in Durham.
>
> (Bishop A. Bek, 1302)

Evidence of former greatness still persists, when at each coronation the Bishop of Durham stands at the right hand of the monarch at the crowning ceremony in Westminster Abbey. It is also worth noting that in place of the royal standard, the flag of St. Cuthbert flies above the castle when the Assize Courts are in session and the judges in residence.

Continue now with the journey the Bishop makes to his cathedral, castle and

Saxon Church, Escomb

city. Head for Durham City on the A688 and turn north on to the old A1 road, the A167.

On the outskirts, at the 'Cock of the North', turn right on to the A1050, South Road, and continue into the heart of the city. But spare some time to look at the University buildings on the way, some by architects such as William Whitfield, Sir Basil Spence and Richard Sheppard. It is only at this point, a mile from the centre, that the full glory of the cathedral becomes apparent, though the best grandstand views are obtained from the windows of the trains rumbling over the viaduct near the railway station.

Durham! The jewel in the crown of the Kingdom of Northumbria. The cathedral and castle are without equal in Europe. Built on a wooded rock high above the river which has wound its way around to form a peninsula. It is a Mecca to tourists, pilgrims and artists. Its cobbled, narrow streets and inadequate vehicle access have protected it from the worst ravages of the planners, though the fact that most of the land and buildings are owned by the cathedral and university has also been a major factor in ensuring its preservation.

Begin your exploration in the market place, by the copper-green statue of the Third Marquess of Londonderry on his prancing steed. The name of this aristocratic colliery owner is not likely to conjure up kind thoughts amongst the miners, and probably no thoughts at all for the rest of us. 'Lord Who?' The miners knew well enough in 1844 when the Marquess went into action against them. He brought in 3,500 blackleg labourers from his Irish Londonderry estates, evicting the striking Durham men and their families from their homes. He also closed the workhouses so that they had nowhere to go, leaving them to camp on waste ground. Shopkeepers were forbidden to provide goods to them, even on credit, and after twenty weeks they crawled back, begging and bitter.

Bishop Auckland Castle

The market place has some charm, the best building being the Town Hall, designed by the architect of the old Euston Station in London. Inside there is some fine stained glass, one window depicting Edward III, the young king, astride a white charger, thanking the citizens of Durham for rescuing his baggage train which had been left unguarded while he fought off the Scots invaders.

Silver Street leads off the market place and meanders its narrow, cobbled way downhill to Framwellgate Bridge, where there was once a mustard mill, the first the world ever knew. Here the cathedral and castle stand in all their splendour, towering above the river which creates a natural moat below them.

The cathedral's defensive characteristics must have been even more obvious in the eighth century when Danish raids were a constant threat to the Anglo-Saxons. At this time, many ancient coastal centres of monasticism were looted and burned, among them Jarrow, Monkwearmouth and Lindisfarne. The Benedictine monastery on Holy Island was at that time the shrine of St. Cuthbert, the shepherd boy who became a monk. He was Bishop of Lindisfarne in 685 AD and died soon after. Ten years later his body was re-examined and found not to have decayed at all, and from this time he was credited, dead or alive, with powers of healing and miracles. The monks had to carry his body with them when they finally left Lindisfarne in 875 AD, and after much nomadic wandering, to Chester-le-Street and Ripon, they brought him to Durham in 995 AD where his coffin lay in a small church made of tree branches until the cathedral was built. The ceremony of the laying of the foundation stone in 1093 was attended by Malcolm III, the King of Scotland who slew Macbeth.

Malcolm: *Nothing in his life*
            Became him like the leaving it: he died
            As one that had been studied in his death
            To throw away the dearest thing he owed
            As 'twere a careless trifle.

(W. Shakespeare)

The spot was chosen by the monks, not just as a defensive bastion, but because of a vision in which they were told to find safety where a girl was milking a dun cow. The realisation of the vision came when they reached Durham and at that moment the coffin became rooted to the ground, immovable. When William the Conqueror came a century later it was still there, but in no mood for piety he attempted to seize and empty the coffin. As he moved towards it he was said to have been overcome with a deadly faintness, which only left him when he climbed on his horse and rode furiously away.

The dun cow incident is commemorated in a carving on the cathedral wall, facing Dun Cow Lane, but St. Cuthbert's miracle-working powers live on even today. Indeed, many believe that during the 1939–45 war, each time German bombers approached Durham, St. Cuthbert drew down a thick mist, diverting the aircraft elsewhere!

The cathedral was completed in 1133 and St. Cuthbert laid to rest in a tomb behind the high altar. His body had been examined in 1104 and again in 1540, before witnesses, and was still to be found uncorrupted, with no sign of decay. Only the black oak coffin had decayed, and its remains were placed with St. Cuthbert in a new coffin.

However, a disbelieving Protestant divine in 1827, anxious to disprove the

Durham City

story, opened the coffin and found only a broken skeleton and relics. In triumph he proclaimed his discovery, but had he opened the correct coffin? Not if we are to believe the story still current and set down in verse by Sir Walter Scott:–

There deep in Durham's gothic shade
His relics are in secret laid,
But none may know the place
Save of his holiest servants three,
Deep sworn to solemn secrecy,
Who share that wondrous grace.

The story still lingers on that the true location of St. Cuthbert's uncorrupted body is hidden in the cathedral and the spot known only to the Prior of the Roman Catholic monks at nearby Ushaw College. It is possible that it could be true, especially as his gold and sapphire ring rifled in 1538 turned up there later.

Cuthbert was known to have been averse to the company of women and it was the rule that no woman should approach his shrine. One who did, inadvertently, was Queen Philippa, wife of Edward III. On discovering her error, she was in such a state of fear that she left the Prior's Lodge, where she was staying, in the middle of the night with nothing on but a cloak, and fled down Dun Cow Lane entreating the saint not to avenge the fault she had committed.

It is not unknown for people who live on the Peninsula to be struck with religious and aggressive fervour beyond the bounds of sanity. However St. Cuthbert has grown with the times; historians deny his prejudices, and certainly it is true that both men and women stand over and on his tomb with no obvious

113

harm. Some even swear that a prayer on this spot can cure the ills that afflict mankind. Try it!

But first pass over Framwellgate Bridge, turning left and left again to climb ancient South Street which runs parallel with the river, but high above it. The fine array of gentlemen's townhouses testifies to the importance of the street, quite apart from its splendid views across the river. This was the old coach route from London to Edinburgh and is such a fine street that it is hard to take in the stupendous scene, known to the connoisseur but missed by most tourists.

Upon the wooded hill across the Wear stands the bastion of the castle with its castellated towers and keep, separated from the three towers of the mighty cathedral by a twentieth century masterpiece in stone, the University Library designed by George Pace. This western view of the peninsula is an endless vista of dynamic architecture and nature – breathtaking and ineffable. The tiny Galilee Chapel can only been seen with difficulty. It houses the tomb of the great saint and historian, the Venerable Bede, who died at the monastery in Jarrow in 735 AD after writing his great *History of the English Church and People*, still published today as a paperback.

To the Most Glorious King Ceolwulf
from Bede the Priest and Servant of Christ

Some while ago, at Your Majesty's request, I gladly sent you the history of the English Church and People which I had recently completed, in order that you might read it and give it your approval.

For if history records good things of good men, the thoughtful bearer is encouraged to imitate what is good: or if it records evil of wicked men, the devout, religious listener or reader is encouraged to avoid all that is sinful and perverse and to follow what he knows to be good and pleasing to God.

His bones were stolen from Jarrow, and after a series of strange goings-on were brought to Durham with many relics in 1370.

At the end of South Street, opposite Grove Street, go through the snicket in the wall and follow the path downwards on the banks of the river to Prebends Bridge. There is no finer part of the Wear than this, with the golden hue of Prebends arched bridge, towering sycamores and beeches, leaning alders and . . . silence and serenity everywhere. Sublime symmetry framed by immortal hand and eye.

Look, two and two go the priests, then the monks with
cowls and sandals.
And the penitents dressed in white shirts, a-holding the
yellow candles;
One, he carries a flag up straight, and another a cross
with handles,
And the Duke's guard brings up the rear, for the better
prevention of scandals:
BANG, WHANG, WHANG goes the drum, TOOTLE-TE-TOOTLE
the fife,
Oh, a day in the city square, there is no such pleasure in life!

(Robert Browning)

Durham Castle and Cathedral

Across the bridge in the 'Bailey' lies a wealth of Georgian and Queen Anne architecture, though most visitors pay more attention to the brass horse knocker on the door of No. 27. Enjoy the bubbling life of the university and the cathedral as you walk. St. Cuthbert's Society, St. John's College, St. Chad's, Hatfield, and a tempting glimpse through an ancient stone archway of the Dean's preserve, 'The College'. It was here that John Balliol, founder of Balliol College, Oxford, and then Lord of Barnard Castle, was publicly flogged for his misdemeanours, on the orders of the Bishop of Durham exercising his regal powers.

Go on past the great rose window of the cathedral. Dun Cow Lane on the left, Bow Lane on the right, leading to Ove Arup's spectacular high-level footbridge. Continue on, the great moment is coming. Turn left up Owengate. If you can bear to turn your eyes you will see some of the oldest houses in Durham, four hundred years old, but you may be forgiven for missing them. For me they represent a part of my life – seventeen years spent at the university, rescuing, restoring and replacing a part of the old city – the major part – from castle to college, from ancient sandstone to modern brick, some with foundations, some with none at all. The blood, toil, tears and satisfaction embedded in the mortar are mine, though not mine alone. Bernard Taylor, the architect who has produced the black and white illustrations for this book, also played a prominent part in the restoration of the ancient buildings.

Suddenly the cathedral bursts forth in its full magnificence as you approach Palace Green. Castle and library to the right, almshouses to the left, but the green sward ahead is the perfect foreground for this incredible view of the Cathedral Church of St. Mary the Virgin – without equal and beyond the power of human words to justly praise. Savour it to the full, and then go forward and place your hand on the twelfth century bronze Santuary Knocker with its grotesque head and ringed mouth. Fugitives from the law could claim protection once they laid hand on it, and it is recorded that 331 people did so between 1464 and 1524.

Inside, the nave is vast. Huge pillars, deeply cut in rugged patterns of spiral, flute, lozenge and chevron, Norman arches seventy feet high, the Chapel of Nine Altars, the Galilee and Gregory Chapels, St. Cuthbert, St. Bede – all are there. The Bishop is there too, in the form of his throne, elevated to be the highest in Christendom! And the miners? Their wall memorial in black Spanish oak pleads:–

> Remember before God the Durham miners who have given their lives in the pits of the county, and who work in darkness and danger in those pits today.

Remember, too a former Prior of the cathedral by the name of John Washington (1416–1446) whose family gave rise to the first President of the United States of America. On the cathedral wall in a corner of the cloisters is a plaque with the words:–

> Remember in these cloisters which were finished in his day John Washington of Washington in this County, Prior of this Cathedral 1416–1446, whose family has won an everlasting renown in lands to him unknown.

Off the South Transept, there can be found the Durham Light Infantry Chapel where the tattered standards of that regiment hang, faded and fragile. Often forgotten, the deeds and courage of the Durham soldiers remind us of the sacrifice these young men made:–

118

As such peace and prosperity prevail in these days, many of the Northumbrians, both noble and simple, together with their children, have laid aside their weapons. What the result of this will be the future will show.

(Bede)

The altar screen of white Caen stone, one of the most elaborate ever seen, was made in 1375 in London, brought to Newcastle and erected at the expense of Lord John Neville, son of the victor of the battle at Nevilles' Cross against the Scots – as decisive a battle as Flodden – on the western outskirts of Durham. The 107 alabaster statues it once held were destroyed in the Reformation. The Nevilles of Raby Hall might well have grasped the throne of England, but unwisely chose to join the Catholic rebellion against the government of Queen Elizabeth which came to nought.

Now was the North in arms: they shine
In warlike trim from Tweed to Tyne
At Percy's voice: and Neville sees
His followers gathering in from Tees,
From Wear, and all the little rills
Concealed among the forkéd hills –
Seven hundred knights, Retainers all
Of Neville, at their master's call
Had sate together in Raby hall!

(William Wordsworth)

119

There have been skirmishes in the cathedral too, at least one involving the third Lord Neville. He demanded that he and his retinue should be entertained to dinner by the Prior and sent his servants ahead with a stag. On being told that the Prior was too busy, they laid the stag on St. Cuthbert's tomb, whereupon the monks attacked them with heavy candlesticks.

The marble altar of 1630 has unfortunately seen, even recently, at least one human sacrifice on it, and one lesser human folly in the cathedral was the replacement of Bishop Cosin's oak choir screen with Sir Gilbert Scott's marble monstrosity. It should be removed, but the cry goes up, 'Replaced with what?' To which the answer plainly is, 'Nothing.'

There are treasures in the Monks' Dormitory such as St. Cuthbert's coffin, pectoral cross, gold studded with garnets, and stole of great antiquity. There are treasures everywhere in this cathedral, yet I once overheard a visitor say as she left, 'Ah well, when you've seen one, you've seen them all!'

Just examine the huge pillars, each twenty-two feet in circumference, and their various carvings, all prefabricated. Examine the rich vaultings and the concealed buttresses. If breath allows, take the steps by the astronomical clock (1500 AD) to the top of the tower, where once a year the choir sings from the roof. Also, why not sit a while in the choir stalls and listen to Evensong – the music may be three hundred years old – but it is the best way to experience this amazing building.

The Choristers' School, the Monks' Refectory, the Deanery – all should be viewed – and for refreshment the well designed visitors' refectory.

Incidentally, when the new underfloor central heating system was installed in the cathedral a few years ago, stains appeared on the stone flags accompanied by a strange smell – ammonia, to put it politely. The late Dr Whitworth, Master of Hatfield College and Palaeontologist, put forward the theory that it was urine from the four thousand Scottish prisoners kept there in 1650 after the battle of Dunbar. Cromwell herded them into the cathedral, half-starved and exhausted, and many died as a result. The smell of history is here.

The modern architect whose imprint is left on the cathedral is George Pace, alas dead. His work appears in many great cathedrals. There is no better example of his restoration work than the Galilee Chapel, a place of homage, where Norman architecture and modern restoration meld with the remains of the Venerable Bede to provide a feeling of human pride in great and famous men.

Bede is of the greatest importance to English history for, born in 673 AD, he was the Father of English Learning. In all, he wrote seventy-nine books on everything that was known at that time of mathematics, physics, astronomy, music, medicine and philosophy. His wealth of knowledge, mostly self-taught, was phenomenal. One of his essays on Time ran to two hundred pages. He lived until 735 AD and was still writing, though too weak to hold a pen. The day he died he gave away his few possessions and hastened to finish his translation of the Gospel of St. John, urging his boy scribe to write faster. The boy finally called out to him, 'One sentence, dear master, is left unfinished.' The old man summoned up his strength and gave him the translation. 'It is finished,' said the boy, and Bede replied, 'True, it is finished,' and closing his eyes, he died.

Once a year these words are read to commemorate the Founders and Benefactors of cathedral and university alike:–

> Let us now praise famous men, and our fathers that begat us. The Lord hath wrought great glory by them through his great power from the beginning. Such as did bear rule in their kingdoms, men renowned for their power, giving counsel by their understanding, and declaring prophecies: leaders of the people by their counsels, and by their knowledge of learning meet for the people, wise and eloquent in their instructions: such as found out

Durham Castle

musical tunes, and recited verses in writing: rich men furnished with ability, living peaceably in their habitations: all these were honoured in their generations, and were the glory of their times. There be of them, that have left a name behind them, that their praises might be reported. And some there be, which have no memorial; who are perished, as though they had never been; and are become as though they had never been born.

(Ecclesiasticus)

When you leave the cathedral walk slowly to the castle, built in the twelfth century, although added to since, by and for the Bishops; the Prince Bishops of the Palatinate, rulers by right with their own armies. In 1640 during the Civil War it was captured by the Scots and held for nearly a year. When it was later confiscated by Cromwell from the Bishops it was sold off to the Lord Mayor of London for £1267. Bishop Cosin re-acquired it in 1660, when he repaired and added to it. So strongly did he feel about his office of Prince Bishop that he demanded that a whale washed ashore at Easington be brought to him, where he kept it beneath the castle keep. In 1839 the skeleton was rediscovered and the bones transferred to the cathedral crypt, where they can still be seen.

The University of Durham was founded in 1832 and the castle handed over to it, where it now houses University College, the senior Durham college. The castle is a mixture of styles, but its real gem is not the Great Hall or the Black Staircase but the Norman Chapel, restored to its original form. The piers of local sandstone, beautifully and strongly veined, are a brilliant gold hue and the Norman sculpture of the capitals shows grotesque figures, animals, plants and geometrical designs. The herringbone flagstones in the central aisle are over a thousand years old.

The Senate Room, together with the adjoining Judges' rooms is especially interesting. The 400-year-old mantel with arms of Scotland and England commemorates the visit of James VI of Scotland on his way south to become James I of England.

It was during the Reformation that a university in Durham was first proposed and Oliver Cromwell went so far as to issue the Letters Patent making over the cathedral and other properties. Unfortunately, Cromwell's power came to an end and it was not until 1832 that the idea was revived by Bishop Van Mildert, who donated the castle for its use. Whether this was entirely philanthropic or whether it was because the castle was in a state of collapse – it nearly fell into the river later – none can say, but at any rate a start was made and a century and a half later, having expanded south of the river and into the Elvet area, it had 4,500 students. The university has contributed in no small way to the wealth of academic and practical achievement in such diverse fields as theology, geology and physics. Its new buildings, too, are ahead of any university in the land, with numerous architectural and Civic Trust awards to its credit. A tour of the university grounds and buildings is an exciting experience in itself, of which the architects and institution can be justly proud.

Dame Margot Fonteyn is its present Chancellor, while recent incumbents of the post have included Sir Malcolm MacDonald (son of Ramsey) among their number. But no one has contributed more to the university's success than Sir Derman Christopherson, FRS, its Vice-Chancellor in the 'sixties and 'seventies.

Among the recipients of its honorary degrees, who have processed from the castle to the cathedral on Congregation Day, are William Wordsworth (poet), Charles Chaplin and Dame Freya Stark (intrepid explorer). Freya, born in 1893 and still exploring, might have said of Durham, as she did gazing up at the peaks of Annapurna:–

The awe and majesty of this last approach; the last terrestrial footsteps to infinity . . . I sit in the shadows but I look at the light.

If time permits, walk down Dun Cow Lane and Bow Lane past the Master's Lodgings of Hatfield College to Ove Arup's modern footbridge and visit Durham's other great institution, the gaol, whose maximum security wing has held, and still holds, the evil and reformed alike.

Return by Old Elvet and Elvet Bridge to the market place, passing Magdalen Steps and the old butchers' row, Fleshergate. Close by, behind the 'Buffalo Head' in Saddler Street, a seventh century timber stockade settlement was found intact when the foundations of a new student residence were being excavated. The stockade was buried under tons of leather off-cuts from the workings of the shoe- and saddle-makers who worked in Saddler Street. Higher up the street, in North Bailey, the skeletal remains of bodies were also discovered (one beneath the floor of Hatfield College in what can only be described as suspicious circumstances) in the old Jevons House. This was regarded as the property of the University of Dublin(!) at one time and later as the home of John Gully, Member of Parliament, innkeeper, butcher, prize fighter and gaol bird – as well as father of twenty-four children and husband to two wives!

You will not have exhausted the possibilities that are Durham; it will have exhausted you. If time is short, leave Palace Green by Windy Gap, a vennel running between the University Library and the Music School. Then turn right for a delightful stroll through the wooded banks beneath the castle walls to Framwellgate Bridge. You have finished the exploration, but . . . return . . . again and again, to see more of its ancient splendour.

Our journey ends here, but you may wish to follow the River Wear to

Monkwearmouth where it meets the North Sea – Monkwearmouth, the old monastic site where St. Bede was born; Sunderland (Sundered-land), the town where ships and football once reigned supreme.

On the way there is Finchale Abbey, the ruins of a thirteenth century Benedictine monastery on the river, and not far away is Washington Old Hall, a National Trust property restored with funds from the United States. It once belonged to the family of George Washington (Wessyngton), the first President of the United States. The deed of sale is preserved in the Cathedral Library and the subsequent history of the Washington family after they emigrated to America needs no comment, but one. In all my years in Durham I had never known the people of Northumbria to be gripped by the personality cult, royal or otherwise, yet the welcome given to President Jimmy Carter when he visited the area on 6 May 1977 was little short of ecstatic and inexplicable, for it was as if the link in the minds of the people with the first President of the United States had never been broken.

Galilee Chapel

CHAPTER FIVE

Low Force

TUMBLING TEESDALE

TUMBLING TEESDALE

YARM – CROFT – BARNARD CASTLE – MIDDLETON – COW GREEN
(Distance 65 miles)

'Vltava' from 'My Country'
Smetana

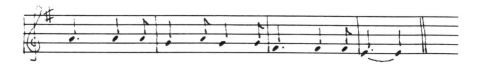

'Life without industry is guilt'

(John Ruskin)

 Each dale in Northumbria has a unique character and, unlike their Yorkshire counterparts, these dales have within them contrasts so extreme that they can scarcely be believed. Looking at the swirling, polluted estuary of the Tees, once dominated by the steel and chemical industries and now by dereliction and unemployment, it is impossible to imagine that this same river could be the spring of such beauty and timelessness as it trickles, then tumbles, down from the hills that form the backbone of England.

Until recently Teesside (now Cleveland) lived and died by heavy industry, yet the River Tees itself flows from the Pennines to the North Sea through a valley as strangely seductive and beautiful as any other in the land. Early in the nineteenth century forty-eight lead and coal mines were operating in Teesdale, yet the same conditions of weather and soil that produced the minerals underground also produced and nurtured the rare alpine flowers that flourish here. Over fifty plants have been recorded, including the lovely spring gentian, the alpine forget-me-not, lady's mantle and yellow mountain saxifrage. Not surprisingly it is called 'Little Switzerland' as botanists wax lyrical over the soil in which sugar limestone has crumbled the clay to form an ideal compost.

Industrial giants like ICI and British Steel have turned the other end of the Tees into a weird robotic universe, lit night and day by yellow sodium lamps in order to produce fertilisers, foodstuffs for animals, steel for armaments and ships.

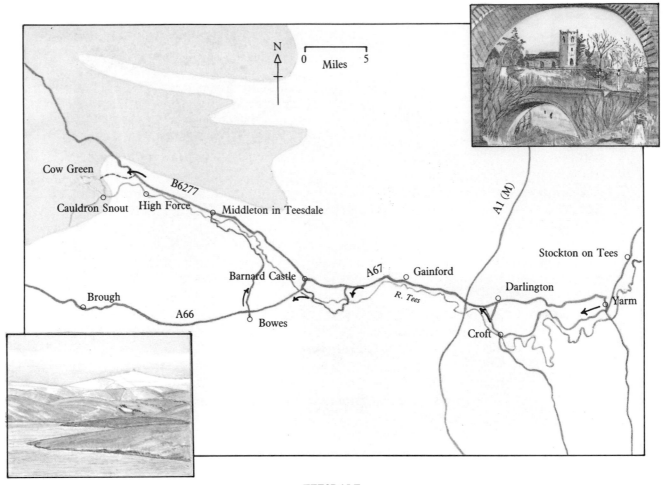

N
△

0 Miles 5

Cow Green

B6277

Cauldron Snout   High Force   Middleton in Teesdale

A1 (M)

Stockton on Tees

Barnard Castle   A67   Gainford   Darlington

R. Tees   Yarm

Brough

A66   Bowes   Croft

TEESDALE

Tumbling Teesdale

The fear that kills;
And hope that is unwilling to be fed;
Cold, pain, and labour, and all fleshly ills;
And mighty Poets in their misery dead.
– Perplexed, and longing to be comforted,
My question eagerly I did renew.
'How is it that you live, and what is it you do?'

(William Wordsworth)

It is a place of pilgrimage, too, for railway enthusiasts who come to see George Stephenson's *Locomotion*, the first railway engine in the world to pull a passenger train – from Stockton to Darlington in 1825. A pilgrimage also for lovers of *Alice in Wonderland*, for Lewis Carroll was nurtured here. And who wouldn't come to see Dotheboys Hall, the Bowes school so devastatingly described by Dickens in *Nicholas Nickleby*?

Make this journey in spring if possible, to see the alpine plants in flower. That's the climax to this exploration, but we begin at Yarm where the North Sea tide meets the lonely river.

Enclosed in a loop of the Tees, Yarm is a mirror of the Durham peninsula, but in no way so dramatic. Its single main street runs north–south carrying the A67. The high street widens to form a market place with its Dutch-style eighteenth century Town Hall as the centrepiece. Built by the Lord of the Manor, Viscount Fauchonberg, it has suffered the indignity of having its arches bricked up to provide much needed public conveniences. It has been said before that the people of Yarm are strangely reticent in giving away information to visitors except

Yarm

regarding the number of pubs, about which they have no inhibitions, but in a town with so much history they hardly know where to begin.

Walk south, then turn down towards the river at Atlas Wynd by the Friarage school built in 1770 on the site of a Dominican Friary founded in 1260. The Wynd runs along the edge of Atlas Skinnery where sheepskins are washed and treated – a trade called fell mongering. Tanning is a traditional industry of Yarm, once carried on in a number of small houses and yards. Now Atlas, as its name implies, has swallowed them up and a factory has engulfed the surrounding warehouses and mills.

Through the trees on the right the old Friary's Dovecote can still be seen and on reaching the river bank you arrive at the harbour, which in the eighteenth century was a bustling, thriving port exporting the products of Teesdale – agricultural goods, lead, cotton, hides, timber, coal – to France, Scotland and the Baltic. Even in the stillness that now prevails you can see the images of sailing ships and lighters against the background of chandlers, warehouses, matelots, inns and twenty windmills between Yarm and the sea.

Along the footpath you have excellent views of Yarm's famous bridge, built in 1400. Though much liable to flooding, it has withstood the pressure of the elements.

The morning was beautifully calm, and the view from the high ground at Egglescliffe was singularly grand. The Tees had become an immense silver lake in which boats were plying, and in the midst of which the town of Yarm seemed immersed.

(Ord, 1822)

The Tees was a difficult river to navigate, with its shifting sands and channels, but despite this Yarm flourished for six hundred years as a port, so much so that customs dues were £43, compared with £20 at Stockton and only 4*s*. at Scarborough. Its demise came when the building of larger ships meant that they could no longer navigate the shallow waters to Yarm and so transferred their trade to Stockton.

The superb 600-year-old stone-arch bridge, built by Bishop Skirlaw as a toll bridge, must have reaped the Bishop of Durham and his successors much reward. It was closed from Saturday night to Sunday night to keep out drunken drivers, but a local printer wrote in 1777:—

> During Sunday nights, coal carts drew up in large numbers waiting for the bridge to open and many lively scenes occurred when drivers tried to secure the best positions. When the barrier was withdrawn the heterogeneous collection of horses and donkeys drawing wagons and carts etc., rushed off at their best pace for the Durham coalfields, as those arriving first were first served.

A wider iron bridge was built alongside in 1820 but was promptly washed away, its abutments having collapsed, and so, with broader approaches added, the old bridge remains, providing the only way out of Yarm and carrying twenty thousand vehicles per day.

Beyond the bridge along 'True Lovers' Walk' is the railway viaduct bisecting the peninsula and dominating Yarm. Built in 1849, the viaduct carries the main line from London to Middlesbrough and spans half a mile.

The people of Yarm were in the main protected from the Scottish marauders, but there were bitter feelings towards King Robert Bruce who looted and burned

137

the town five times between 1312 and 1322. The Archbishop of York ordered his excommunication, but it mattered not to Robert Bruce, who returned each time to a hero's welcome in Scotland, bringing with him the booty he had stolen from the church and the people of Yarm and leaving behind a trail of misery amongst those whose crops he had destroyed.

The townspeople were strongly Catholic in faith, six of them being hanged for their loyalty in the market place during the Reformation. The Friars were driven out, the altar plate transferred to the king's jewelhouse and the Friary sold for £79. 10s.

From the centre of Yarm, drive north over Yarm bridge into Egglescliffe and take the first turning left before the traffic lights, signposted to Aislaby, and then across the railway bridge. As the road curves to Aislaby there is a wonderful view of the long Yarm viaduct and the west side of the town below it.

Beyond Aislaby the land is flat and the road full of twists and turns, but interest is heightened by glimpses over the hedgerows of planes taxiing, taking off and landing at Teesside Airport. During the Second World War the airport at Middleton-St.-George was the only bomber station north of the Tees. The Royal Canadian Air Force flew from here in their Lancasters and Halifaxes.

Outside Low Middleton Hall is a sign indicating the boundary between the (new) county of Cleveland and County Durham. The Hall itself is in brick with a pantile roof and extensive outbuildings, including an eight-sided pigeon house with fifteen hundred nesting holes.

The approach to Middleton One Row is marked by an array of lights at the end of the runway. The village is reminiscent of a Victorian seaside resort with houses and hotels on a curve of elegant proportions overlooking the wooded banks of the Tees.

The road turns sharp right away from the river into Middleton-St.-George past the church of St. Lawrence, and then follows the signposted route to Hurworth and Croft, turning left at Dinsdale railway station. The river is out of sight, away to the left, but from here it is possible to see over the chemical plants and cooling towers to the Cleveland hills beyond. To the right is the industrial fringe of Darlington above the low and flat 'Hurworth Moor'. Much of the road is lined with fine old trees on both sides before it drops down to Neasham.

As a diversion, there is a house a short distance along the incoming road from Low Dinsdale called 'Neasham Hill', with a plaque dating it 'c.1757:– Gardens open daily 2–5.30 p.m.'. Low Dinsdale is well worth exploring, with its single track steel bridge, Over Dinsdale Hall and Dinsdale Park, now a residential school. The gnarled ivy-covered tree trunks seem to have been there forever.

Continue on the main road until you reach the beautiful and elegant Hurworth, past the 'Otter and Fish' with a neat row of pantiled, brick terraced houses – Strait Lane – and All Saints Church, which has an unusual covered lych gate incorporating church pews on either side, for all the world like an ecclesiastical bus shelter.

Beyond the squat towered church is the 'Bay Horse', an attractive little pub with an enclosed yard. There are many fine double-fronted houses, one with a sun-dial, along the widened street which leads directly into Croft-on-Tees, dropping down to the bridge across the London–Edinburgh main railway line and curving into Croft.

Our route turns right on to the A167 – signed Darlington – but first explore Croft by crossing the bridge at the pub called 'Comet' – but why does the inn sign portray an enormous bull? Croft bridge, with its seven-pointed arches linking Yorkshire and Northumbria, has its origins in antiquity, but the present

139

structure is thought to have been built at the same time as Yarm bridge in 1400 by Bishop Skirlaw.

Newly appointed Bishops of Durham were presented with the Conyer's falchion (the broadsword used to kill the voracious serpent, the Sockburn Worm, which terrorised the neighbourhood until killed by Sir John Conyers) with these words:–

> My Lord Bishop, I here present you with the falchion wherewith the champion Conyers slew the worm, dragon, or fiery flying serpent which destroyed man, woman, and child; in memory of which the king then reigning gave him the manor of Sockburn, to hold by this tenure, that upon the first entrance of every bishop into the county the falchion should be presented.

The falchion was returned by the Bishop wishing the Lord of the Manor health, long life and prosperity. The ceremony was last carried out by Van Mildert, the founder of Durham University, in 1826.

But it is to another ecclesiastic that Croft bears the greatest witness. The Reverend Charles Dodgson (we met the name in an earlier chapter), Vicar of Croft, was a distinguished scholar, taking a double first at Christ Church, Oxford, in Classics and Mathematics. In 1828 be married his cousin, Frances Jane Lutwidge, and they had eleven children, four boys and seven girls, Charles Lutwidge Dodgson being the third child and eldest son. The family moved to Croft in 1843 and lived in the spacious rectory. It was this eldest boy, Charles, who, as Lewis Carroll, became the creator of *Alice in Wonderland*. When the family moved to Croft, Charles was eleven years old, dark-haired, dreamy-eyed and with a marked speech stammer. It was here that he began writing and producing magazines for the family and parish, with poems, stories and sketches. One of his first poems, written in mock protest at the conduct of the Rectory, was called 'Rules and Regulations':–

> *Shut doors behind you,*
> *(Don't slam them, mind you.)*
> *Write well and neatly,*
> *And sing most sweetly.*
> *Learn well your grammar,*
> *And never stammer.*
> *Eat bread with butter,*
> *Once more, don't stutter.*

After three miserable years of being educated at Rugby School, he returned to Croft and wrote, 'I cannot say that I look back on my life at a Public School with any sensations of pleasure, or that any earthly considerations would induce me to go through my three years again.'

He used to wander along the Tees sketching and making notes. Croft was an interesting place then, with one of the best coaching inns in the north, the 'Croft Spa'. The mineral waters were bottled and sold in London like a modern day Perrier.

> *Fair stands the ancient Rectory*
> *The Rectory of Croft,*
> *The sun shines bright upon it,*
> *The breezes whisper soft.*

141

——————————————————— ———

From all the house and garden
Its inhabitants come forth,
And muster in the road without,
And pace in two and threes about,
The children of the North.

He left for Oxford, but within two days was back again when his mother collapsed and died. He wrote:–

Here may the silent tears I weep,
Lull the vexed spirit into rest,
As infants sob themselves to sleep
Upon a mother's breast.

The origins of many of his characters were in the north. *The Walrus and the Carpenter* was conceived in Whitby. Curious carvings of strange beasts appear on the church furniture at Croft, and in Beverley he found his white rabbit carved on the door of St. Mary's Church. *Jabberwocky* was written at Whitburn near Sunderland.

'Twas brillig and the slithy toves
Did gyre and gimble in the wabe:
All mimsy were the borogoves,
And the mome raths outgrabe.

142

The strange words owed much to the legends of Croft, the Sockburn Worm and falchion. 'It's very pretty but hard to understand,' says Alice, to which Humpty Dumpty replied, 'brillig means four o'clock in the afternoon – slithy means lithe and slimy. Toves are something like badgers, and lizards – and corkscrews too. To gyre is to go round and round like a gyroscope, and to gimble is to make holes like a gimlet. A wabe is a grass plot around a sun-dial, and mimsy is flimsy and miserable. A borogove is a thin shabby-looking bird, mome is short for home, raths are sorts of green pigs, and outgrabing is something between bellowing and whistling.'

Later in this journey we visit Dotheboys Hall at Bowes. Lewis, on holiday in 1856, wrote:–

> We set out by coach for Barnard Castle at about seven, and passed over about forty miles of the dreariest hill-country I ever saw; the climax of wretchedness was reached at Bowes where yet stands the original of 'Dotheboys Hall'; it has long ceased to be used as a school and is falling into ruin, in which the whole place seems to be following its example – the roofs are falling in, and the windows broken or barricaded – the whole town looks plague-stricken. The courtyard of the inn we stopped at was grown over with weeds, and a mouthing idiot lolled against the corner of the house, like the evil genius of the spot. Next to a prison or a lunatic asylum preserve me from living at Bowes!

Carroll and Alice were a product of the combined effect of Croft and Oxford – the latter is always remembered, the former hardly at all. He died in 1898 at Guildford.

The A167 going out of Croft towards Darlington crosses the River Skerne which has wound its way through the great railway town to flow into the Tees. The road here is fast, and if there is little to notice it is because the countryside is in transition from soft plain to the foothills. Join the A67 signposted for Barnard Castle and flash through Low Conniscliffe, over the A1 to Merrybent and High Conniscliffe, with the river on the left.

Piercebridge is famous for its Roman origins, though you may, like me, find the remains invisible. But our old friend Dere Street, the Roman road, is not. The main artery to Hadrian's Wall from York and London must have been a great deal busier then than it is now. Enjoy a drink by the large open fire at the George Hotel.

Continue on to Gainford, 'esteemed for its picturesque and salubrious character', though its chief claim to fame, especially since the BBC portrayed the story on television, is the Lizzie Pearson tale.

In March 1875, just when the people of Gainford were recovering from the stresses of a hard winter, shock waves hit the small village and reverberated through the country. James Watson, who lived in a cottage along Low Green in the centre of the village, died from what was at first thought to be pneumonia, but after a post-mortem was found to be strychnine poisoning. Eventually his niece Lizzie Pearson, who acted as his housekeeper, was charged and convicted of the murder on the circumstantial grounds that she had obtained rat poison from the local shop. Lizzie, protesting her innocence to the last, was hanged at Durham Gaol. George Smith, James Watson's lodger, was present at his death and then disappeared without trace and was never heard of again, but the possibility of his being the murderer cut no ice with the jury. Lizzie was described as 'unattractive, reticent, morbid-minded and a creature gifted with little that would find favour with those around her.' In prison she claimed she was 'enciente' – with child – but to no avail. She clung to the hope that her life would be spared and continued to maintain her innocence.

Two men were hanged with her, all three deemed to be murderers.

On Monday August 2nd, 1875, they were up and dressed shortly before 6 a.m., fully two hours before they were to be executed. Up to 7 a.m. it appears they were beset with clergymen in prayers for a whole hour. Then they were served with breakfast of a mutton chop with tea and buttered white bread while the warders enjoyed brandies.

About 16 minutes before 8 a.m. the order came for their removal to the press room where they were pinioned by the executioner. They were then conducted to the scaffold which had been erected in a spot between the ends of the male and female wings. Mrs. Pearson who continued to show the utmost composure, was placed with her back to the two men in the centre of the outside beam. At 8 o'clock the executioner put caps over his victims' heads, and then fully two and a half minutes elapsed before he raised the lever and the folding doors fell from behind the prisoners.

That is not the end of the story, for to this day there are reports of inexplicable wailings and the sound of footsteps in James Watson's house, and Lizzie's child, born in prison, appears in the census taken seven years later.

Life, What is it but a Dream?

Long has paled that sunny sky:
Echoes fade and memories die:
Autumn frosts have slain July.

Still she haunts me, phantomwise
Alice moving under skies
Never seen by waking eyes.

Children, yet, the tale to hear,
Eager eye and willing ear,
Lovingly shall nestle near.

In a Wonderland they lie,
Dreaming as the days go by,
Dreaming as the summers die:

Ever drifting down the stream –
Lingering in the golden gleam –
Life, what is it but a dream?

(Lewis Carroll)

Chastened, we drive onwards until we reach the turning to the left marked Whorlton. Most travellers drive on to Barnard Castle, but not the followers of this book. Drive down to Whorlton Bridge and you approach the narrow suspension bridge across the Tees by a one-in-seven incline on a hairpin bend! The setting of the slender bridge between the wooded banks is an unforgettable experience. Downstream of the bridge the river is shallow and fast-flowing over the rocks, much used in summer by canoeists. There is also a picnic park and a model steam railway.

Turn right at Greta Bridge, now by-passed by a new road to the north. Dickens records his arrival at Greta Bridge and the Morritt Arms in these words:–

Barnard Castle

'As we came further north, the snow grew deeper. About eight o'clock it began to fall heavily, and as we crossed the wild heaths hereabout, there was no vestige of a track. The Mail kept on well, however, and at eleven we reached a bare place with a house standing alone in the midst of a dreary moor, which the Guard informed us was Greta Bridge. I was in a perfect agony of apprehension, for it was fearfully cold and there were no outward signs of anybody being up in the house.

To our great joy we discovered a comfortable room with drawn curtains and a most blazing fire. In half an hour they gave us a smoking supper and a bottle of mulled port and then we retired to a couple of capital bedrooms in each of which was a rousing fire half-way up the chimney.'

Dickens continued on the same route as ourselves, the A66. There is a right-hand turn signed for Barnard Castle, Bowes Museum and Eggleston Abbey. On the right is Rokeby Hall, a lovely spot but nowhere to park safely. Egglestone Abbey, now in ruins, was founded in 1195 and is an extravagance of ancient remains above a wooded ravine and well worth visiting. How did Sir Walter Scott describe it in his poem, *Rokeby*?

> *The reverend pile lay wild and waste,*
> *Profaned, dishonour'd, and defaced,*
> *Through storied lattices no more*
> *In soften'd light the sunbeams pour,*
> *Gilding the Gothic sculpture rich*
> *Of shrine and monument and niche.*

Barnard Castle stands guard over the Tees and takes its name from the castle founded in 1112 by Bernard, son of Guy de Baliol, a Norman knight who fought alongside William the Conqueror at the Battle of Hastings. It is one of the finest market towns of national importance and contains the Bowes Museum, a huge French chateau housing the largest collection of French and Spanish paintings in Britain.

John Bowes, the only son of the Earl of Strathmore, married a French actress and the childless couple created this masterpiece in 1869, though both died before it was completed in 1892. The collection includes Boucher's *Landscape with a Water Mill*, Tiepolo's *Harnessing of the Horses of the Sun*, two large Canalettos and Goya's studies of prison life. A veritable wonderland of art in this remote town is just one of the glories of Teesdale.

The town – 'Barney' to its inhabitants – has a fine octagonal Town Hall and a street called 'The Bank', lined on both sides with Tudor and Georgian houses curving down and round to the river, which is crossed by an Elizabethan bridge built in 1569. The remarkable Tudor Blagroves House where Oliver Cromwell stayed in 1648 has projecting rectangular bay windows on a facade alive with figures of musicians. The mounded castle dominates this end of the town and river. Dickens stayed at the King's Head when researching his material for *Nicholas Nickleby* and Dotheboys Hall.

But step back in time and wallow in this unique town, full of artistic and literary treasures, which has changed little and, as luck would have it, still thrives. Its Army connections, with the Durham Light Infantry and other units, are considerable. As a young soldier the effect of 'Barney' stayed with me and drew me back to Northumbria as soon as I was released from the Forces.

The A66 passes over the bridge and takes a sharp turn left. Drive into Bowes, passing under the new by-pass. A sleepy village, and regular travellers on the by-pass miss the comfort of it.

Dotheboys Hall, Bowes

At the far end of the unremarkable main street is Dotheboys Hall. Compared with Dickens's description, it looks innocent and undistinguished. Controversy raged over the headmaster of Bowes Academy, William Shaw, portrayed in *Nicholas Nickleby* as Wackford Squeers, but Dickens's campaign against the school and others like it in the north was certainly successful.

In the novel, the advertisement for the school was set out in full:–

EDUCATION – At Mr. Wackford Squeers' Academy, Dotheboys Hall, at the delightful village of Dotheboys, near Greta Bridge, in Yorkshire, Youth are boarded, clothed, booked, furnished with pocket money, provided with all necessaries, instructed in all languages, living and dead, mathematics, orthography, geometry, astronomy, trigonometry, the use of the globes, algebra, single stick (if required), writing, arithmetic, fortification, and every other branch of classical literature.

Terms, twenty guineas per annum. No extras, no vacation, and diet unparalleled. Mr. Squeers is in town, and attends daily, from one till four, at the Saracen's Head, Snow Hill.

In his preface to *Nicholas Nickleby*, Dickens wrote:–

Of the monstrous neglect of education in England, and the disregard of it by the State as a means of forming good or bad citizens, and miserable or happy men, private schools long afforded a notable example. Although any man who has proved his unfitness for any other occupation in life, was free, without examination or qualification, to open a school anywhere; although preparation for the functions he undertook, was required in the surgeon who assisted to bring a boy into the world, or might one day assist, perhaps, to send him out of it; in the chemist, the attorney, the butcher, the baker, the candlestick maker; the whole round of crafts and trades, the schoolmaster excepted; and although schoolmasters, as a race, were the blockheads and imposters who might naturally be expected to spring from such a state of things, and to flourish in it; these Yorkshire schoolmasters were the lowest

151

and most rotten round in the whole ladder. Traders in the avarice, indifference, or imbecility of parents, and the helplessness of children; ignorant, sordid, brutal men, to whom few considerate persons would have entrusted the board and lodging of a horse or a dog; they formed the worthy cornerstone of a structure, which for absurdity and a magnificent high-minded laissez-aller neglect, has rarely been exceeded in the world.

To continue the journey along the Tees, retrace your steps to the bridge under the by-pass and take the turning marked Cotherstone, where you join the B6277. The road now climbs above the river, skirting the Army shooting range, to Romaldkirk, regarded as the most attractive of all Teesdale villages and dubbed the 'Cathedral of the Dales'. Between Romaldkirk and Mickleton you get the feeling of Upper Teesdale, with isolated farms dotted about on the moors, those painted white indicating they are part of the Raby Estates.

The origin of this custom is that a former Lord Barnard became lost in bad weather and sought refuge at a lonely farmhouse which he thought he owned, and in return for the hospitality he received there he promised to repair the property. When a hefty bill was delivered some time later, he was angry to learn that that farm was not part of his estates, and decreed that all his farms should be whitewashed annually. Another tale states that he was refused a glass of milk at one farmhouse and decided that in order that he might recognise his tenancies, all his properties should be whitewashed each year.

On the crest of the hill is a swirling mass of Swaledale sheep flowing downhill with sheep dogs in attendance.

Middleton-in-Teesdale is now visible, and the road swings to the right and downwards to cross the Tees. As you enter the main street, spare a glance for the eccentric black and gold cherub on the drinking fountain to the right, erected in commemoration of the Bainbridge family by employees of the London Lead Company in 1877. Bainbridge was the head of the Quaker-owned company which went bankrupt in 1905 when cheaper ores from the continent became available.

On the left is the large Raby Estate Office, from which a significant chunk of Teesdale is managed, and on the right is a privately run Tourist Information Centre with an extensive range of literature about the Dale and Northumbria.

On leaving Middleton the road swings sharply to the left and into wilder, more lonely countryside.

Just past Newbiggin is Bowlees, meaning 'the clearing at the bend of the hills'. Turn to the right, signposted Bowlees picnic area. This is a very well worthwhile stopping place. The old chapel in Bowlees has been converted into a Visitors' Centre, with interesting displays of flora, fauna and minerals.

Follow the footpath across a field into woodland on the north bank of the Tees and you will have a fantastic view of Low Force waterfalls, where the river flows over an outcrop of whin sill forming a picturesque cascade once known as Little Force and Salmon Leap. A few yards downstream is the famous Wynch suspension bridge across the whinstone gorge, nearly swept away by Hurricane Charlie. If you are lucky you will see the odd otter or, at dusk, a badger among the pine trees. Usually you will encounter a number of mice, shrews, voles and the inevitable mole heaps. In the evening the rabbits can be seen leaping and playing, and the curlew and lapwing will dance into view from time to time.

Another footpath from the car park, along the beck, leads to Gibson Cave and Summerhill Force – a great attraction in summer is to stand in the cave behind the waters cascading from above.

Leaving Bowlees, the fields are dotted with yet more whitewashed farm buildings. We now pass through Forest-in-Teesdale.

High Force

Double yellow lines appearing on this country road tell us we are approaching something worth seeing, *and* within easy walking distance of the road – in this case, High Force. The car park is on the right. Cross the road on foot, to the path leading down through the Norway spruce to High Force, past a large sign on which Lord Barnard and his employees deny any responsibility if you fall to your death!

High Force, England's largest waterfall, is Teesdale's best known attraction. The river plunges twenty-one metres in to the dark deep pool below over black marble-like whinstone. Lower layers of shale and limestone have been cut away to form a gorge of magnificent proportions. It is a frightening sight and sound when the river is in spate, unpredictable in its ferocity and dangerous. All the time you can hear the thunder of the force and feel the turbulent air.

North of High Force, as we continue our journey, there is a good view of the moors. Here the Pennine Way crosses the road at Langdon Beck Youth Hostel.

Drop down into Langdon Beck with a sharp bend on to a narrow bridge. Over the bridge turn left to Cow Green. Here, Teesdale is at its wildest and most romantic. The river rushes downwards through magnificent, desolate, unspoilt scenery. You have the feeling now that you are getting close to being at the end of the world. There is a final climb, and then a short descent to the car park at Cow Green Reservoir.

In January it is easy to believe that the North Pole is just up the road, and here one Saturday in August 1986 a temperature of −3°C was recorded! The views extend across uninhabited moorlands to the broad summit of Cross Fell, nearly three thousand feet above where our journey began at Yarm. The reservoir, built in 1970 in the teeth of opposition from conservationists, meant the destruction of alpine plants which had grown undisturbed since the glaciers retreated. Some

155

were nurtured and moved to the Botanical Gardens of Durham University, where my colleague David Bellamy was then a lecturer. They look a sorry sight today in their unfamiliar surroundings in Durham City, but those still remaining between High Force and Cow Green include the spring gentian in profusion, the yellow mountain saxifrage, the globe flower and the melancholy thistle.

If you follow the footpath across Widdybank Fell to Cauldron Snout you will see a 200-yard-long series of cataracts of outstanding beauty, particularly superb when the river is in spate, amid scenery unparalleled for its ruggedness. In the peat bogs, relics of 3000 BC have been left behind, of the extinct Bison and flint weapons of the Middle Stone Age. The rocks themselves date back five hundred million years. Some of the original trees around the river still survive above High Force, especially the ancient birch, ash, hazel, bird cherry and rowan. These in turn protect the wood anemone, common violet and the gentians. Strangely, the only species of butterfly round here is the small heath.

Until 1920 the runs of sea trout and salmon were the best in the country. Now the main resident is the brown trout, and occasionally the eel.

The moors are covered in heather, cotton grass and bilberry and make a wonderful purple ridge-to-ridge fitted carpet in September. The endemic bird is the red grouse, but the golden plover's flowing melody can be heard from spring until the onset of winter. There are yellow wagtails and redshanks lower down the river, and in recent years the buzzard, golden eagle and peregrine have returned to the hills.

High pressure tourism takes its toll, and as the Conservation Trust for the county points out, 'Conservation is much more than a gaggle of elegant reserve signs proclaiming the existence of a National Treasure. It is a community of people, naturalists, country lovers and scientists working together to ensure that everyone knows and realises the importance of our natural landscapes as workshops of evolution.' Enjoy it. Look after it. Love it – but don't smother it!

The end of our journey, and in imagination it could be the end of the world. No better place.

Solitude

I love the stillness of the wood:
I love the music of the rill:
I love to couch in pensive mood
Upon some silent hill . . .

Here from the world I win release,
Nor scorn of men, nor footstep rude,
Break in to mar the holy peace
Of this great solitude . . .

Shall the poor transport of an hour
Repay long years of sore distress –
The fragrance of a lonely flower
Make glad the wilderness?

(Lewis Carroll)

Bowlees